# HOW TO BE A
# BRAIN
# EXECUTIVE

## And Get Sensory Smart!

## A Workbook for Understanding and Managing Sensory Patterns

Kathryn Hamlin-Pacheco, OTR/L

## HOW TO BE A BRAIN EXECUTIVE And Get Sensory Smart!

## A Workbook for Understanding and Managing Sensory Patterns

All marketing and publishing rights guaranteed to and reserved by:

**FUTURE HORIZONS**

(817) 277-0727

(817) 277-2270 (fax)

E-mail: info@fhautism.com

www.fhautism.com

ISBN: 9781957984308

# Dedication

This book is dedicated to all of the kids, families, caregivers, and clinicians who read it. I thought of you as I wrote every word.

# Contents

# Contents

# Foreword for the Reader (Soon to Be Brain Executive)

Hi! Before diving into this book, there are just a few things that you should know.

- This book should be read with a trusted adult—your Chief Advisor. This is someone who knows you well and really cares about you. It could be a parent, a foster parent, a grandparent, an aunt or uncle, a mentor, a coach, or even a therapist. Whoever it is, their job is going to be to help you understand the stuff in the book and what it means for you. Also, they are going to help you use some of the info in the book in your everyday life.

- You may notice that throughout the book there are tiny little numbers after some of the words. These numbers have a match in the back of the book that is next to people's names, dates, and titles of a book or article that they wrote. This is showing that the ideas stated just before the tiny number come from some super-smart scientists. (That's whose name is listed in the back). Science is a big community, and we all share information to make sense out of the complicated ideas that are being discovered and researched. When we are sharing, we give people credit for their original ideas. You don't really have to know the people's names, but when you see the tiny numbers in the book, you can say a quick "thank you!" to the smartie scientists that help you be the best Exec that you can be.

- And most of all, have fun! You are about to read about pizza and pythons and farts, and how your brain thinks about all of this. So get ready to laugh and learn some too.

# Foreword for Parents and Caregivers (AKA Chief Advisor)

While this book is written for kids, is designed to be fun and entertaining, and uses kid-friendly language and illustrations, the concepts presented throughout these pages are big ideas. Ideas that help us learn about who we are, how we act, and even how our brains work. Because of the nature of the information, this book is intended to be read alongside a trusted adult who can provide support and guidance as needed along the journey. As the reader is the "Brain Executive," we refer to you as the "Chief Advisor" through the pages. Here are a few things that you should know:

- Chief Advisors are parents, grandparents, foster parents, mentors, coaches, teachers, and other close caregivers who know the child well. In fact, you are the expert on the child, knowing better than any other person what their daily lives, routines, strengths, and challenges are. It is with this invaluable knowledge that you will support the reader in their journey.

- You don't have to be an expert on sensory processing and modulation to be a Chief Advisor. Much of the information that you need is right here within the pages of this book, craftily written to educate you, as well as the child. You can also visit our website at **brainexecutiveprogram.com** to find additional resources for parents and caregivers.

- Because sensory information influences so much of what we do, there are multiple areas of functioning in which we see sensory integration at work. This book focuses on sensory modulation.

- As you read with your child, offer leading questions and examples from their daily life to help them see and understand their personal sensory patterns. They are at an age where self-awareness is growing, so it is imperative to provide help as needed as they learn this skill.

- It may be helpful to offer reminders and cues to your child during the day, prompting them to think about and apply the concepts presented within the book. It is when the information moves from the pages into their daily lives that it will have a positive impact.

- This program is designed to build independence into your child's ability to notice and manage sensory-based challenges, and as a parent/caregiver you know that fostering independence is an art. Just as you first dressed your child, then helped them dress themselves, then laid out appropriate clothing, and eventually they became independent in dressing, you will need to adjust the amount and ways that you help them understand sensory-based challenges across time. At first they may need more direct help, but notice as they learn and grow and be prepared to help a little less as they learn a little more. Ultimately, we want them to notice when they are experiencing a sensory-based challenge, take a moment to understand what is happening, and then implement strategies as needed.

- You may already know that many kids receive therapy for sensory processing challenges. In fact, your child may already be receiving this kind of support. This book is absolutely designed to help these children, but it also has a wider purpose. *Everyone has a sensory system* designed to take in information from the world around and inside us, and *everyone's sensory systems have specific and unique ways in which they work*. Even more, *everyone experiences sensory-based challenges at times*. This universal experience means that understanding sensory patterns can support anyone's ability to engage in everyday life in a way that maximizes success and participation, which is something that we want for all of our children.

- Knowing if and when to seek professional support for our children can be a difficult process. To support your understanding of this question in regards to sensory-based challenges, you will find it discussed in multiple areas of this book, and most thoroughly addressed on pages 186–187. That being said, this book is not designed to determine whether your child needs direct professional support or to substitute for direct professional support. If you have concerns in this area, I encourage you to read these sections of the book, but I mostly encourage you to ask questions to professionals who know, or can evaluate, your child. Your child's pediatrician or family physician is an excellent starting point. You can also contact local pediatric therapy clinics in your area and even discuss your concerns with your child's teacher and educational staff. I hope that this book is a positive addition to your journey, whether it includes further support or not.

- It is my greatest hope for this book is that you enjoy reading it with your child and that it helps your child and your family to understand sensory patterns in a way that supports everyone's well-being. I am an occupational therapist by trade, and to borrow a phrase from the American Occupational Therapy Association, I hope that this book helps your child "live life to the fullest," because that is what every child deserves. Enjoy the journey!

# Foreword for Clinicians

While this book was written so that it can be used in non-clinical settings, the entire program was conceived to address sensory modulation dysfunction through clinical practice, and the development of this book intentionally retains this capacity. I hope that it is a useful tool for you in treatment as you work to support and move your clients toward success and independence.

As you use this resource in practice, you will surely have many of the answers already that your clients will discover as they read. I encourage you to go through the process with them anyway, helping them to see their sensory patterns for the first time. This process of discovery and development of knowledge is both enlightening and empowering. I also encourage you to incorporate parents and caregivers in this process, so that they can support the child during everyday activities. You can find more resources for caregivers on our website at **brainexecutiveprogram.com**.

The amount of science incorporated throughout this book, addressing sensory modulation in a pediatric population, is expansive. As the science is presented in a child-friendly format, a brief clinical introduction is needed to examine how it fits into the concepts presented across the pages.

To say that sensory integration and modulation are complex is an understatement. While it is clear how sensation affects our daily lives in a multitude of ways, understanding the neural systems and processes through which they do this is difficult, to say the least. The purpose of this book is to present the complex neuroscience of sensory modulation in a manner that is comprehensible and functional for children, helping them to live more fully and successfully through the understanding of their sensory patterns. To do this, the concepts must be not only true representations of the science, but also entertaining, memorable, and applicable ideas. Attaining this goal has required simplification, and sometimes generalization, of concepts. In areas, a complex neural process has needed a fitting and age-appropriate word or phrase to encompass the science, yet retain relatability. Surely, much of this work has relied heavily on the "art of therapy," a concept that is vital in sensory integrative practice.[1]

While merging the neuroscience with age-appropriate concepts for a pediatric population has necessitated a blend of both the art and science of therapy, maintaining the integrity of the science has been a priority throughout the development of this book. In an effort to demonstrate both my commitment to evidence-based practice and the blend of art and science that is reflected in this resource, I have summarized how current evidence applies to the concepts found within this book. You will first see a brief consideration of the complexities of the current science in regards to sensory modulation. Then you will find some of the constructs of the Brain Executive book explained as they relate to these concepts.

### *Summary of Current Evidence as it Applies to the Brain Executive Workbook*

1. Terminology associated with sensory integration, including modulation, has a history of confusion, with definitions differing from one setting to another, one institution to another, and one profession to another.[2,3] Lack of clear and definitive definitions can make concepts related to sensory integration difficult to discuss, as we often lack a common language. In a concept analysis of the term "sensory modulation," Brown, Tse, and Fortune[2] found twenty-one definitions that included six different conceptual themes ranging from sensory modulation as a neurophysiological process, to a process that regulates behavior, to a skill, and finally to an intervention. Clearly there is lack of consensus. The same paper proposes a definition of sensory modulation that encompasses a "twofold process" of regulating and processing sensory stimuli on a neurological level and offering an individual "an opportunity to respond behaviorally."

2. Working from the above definition of modulation that includes a neurological process and behavior,[2] it must be then noted that differentiating between neurophysiological processes and behavior is difficult.[3] Many times, we are making behavioral observations and hypothesizing what is occurring neurologically to contribute to these behaviors.[4,5] This is potentially complicated, as behavior is a complex output of multiple biological functions.

3. Modulation is well defined as a physiological process at a cellular level, involving the enhancement or dampening of neuronal activity in response to various input and demands.[3] While it is less defined at a systems level, we can make a "cautionary link" between the two.[3] A systems level concept of modulation expands from the cellular level to involve numerous brain structures and aspects of the limbic system and other higher-level brain functions, and goes further to encompass networks within the brain.[5,6] The limbic system is viewed to be closely associated with sensory modulation,[6] perhaps in part because it is closely associated with behavior, and behavior is closely associated with sensation.[3] Kilroy, Aziz-Zadeh, and Cermak suggest a direct link between modulation and the limbic system, stating that the limbic system can be "disrupted in a way that impairs sensory modulation" and that research validates A. Jean Ayres' theory that "disrupted modulation of sensory stimuli" is present in emotion-related regions of the brain.[6]

4. Attention, attribution of salience, and modulation are closely linked.[3,5] Again, we find concepts that are difficult to differentiate, partially because of overlap in definition and partially because of the limitations inherent to using observable behaviors as neural indicators. Behaviorally, attending to salient information and "tuning out" non-salient information can be thought of as an output of modulation; however, filtering of sensation, habituation, and sensitization can also be thought of as part of the modulatory process.[5] Lane and colleagues state that "the ability to filter out redundant or unnecessary stimuli has also been hypothesized as an underlying deficit of individuals with poor sensory modulation" and that "sensory hyper-reactivity itself is linked to allocating too much attention to basic external input, while also limiting attention to social cues."[7] In her chapter on sensory modulation, Lane also comments that "the act of balancing excitatory and inhibitory inputs to the CNS and *responding only to those that are relevant* [italics added]" is an aspect of modulation. Green and colleagues[8] found that sensory over-responsiveness is linked to greater connectivity in a neural salience network, which includes the anterior insula, amygdala, cingulate cortex, and dorsolateral prefrontal cortex. They also linked attention to sensory modulation, as the salience networks were found to have increased resting-state connectivity with primary sensory processing regions.

5. Sensory modulation and arousal are also closely linked, with sensation influencing arousal and arousal influencing the experience of sensation. Incoming sensory information that moves through the brainstem implicates the reticular formation, which plays a large role in the mediation of arousal via activation of the cortex in response to sensory stimuli.[3,9] In addition, when one is in an alert and attentive state because the reticular formation has elicited increased cortical arousal levels, the cortex is more receptive to sensory input.[3,9] Thus, there is a complex and reciprocal relationship between sensation and arousal. Bundy and Szklut note that "In general, when children are over-responsive to sensation, they tend toward high arousal," and "under-arousal seems to accompany under-responsivity to sensation."[10]

6. Yet another area in which the terminology and concepts are closely linked and difficult to differentiate is the intersection of registration and modulation. Kilroy, Aziz-Zadeh and Cermak note that Ayres herself "hypothesized that poor sensory registration and modulation impairments are closely linked" and expand upon this idea to state that "research providing evidence for registration impairments also provides evidence for modulation deficits."[6] In fact, the complex schematic developed by leaders in sensory integration research and used throughout the definitive textbook on sensory integration, *Sensory Integration Theory and Practice, 3rd Edition* (2020), uses registration as an indicator of modulation. In addition, we find that Dunn's

conceptual model linking neurological threshold to behavioral responsiveness uses the term "registration" to describe a sub-type of sensory modulation dysfunction.[12] Parham and Mailloux note that the term *sensory registration* has been used to describe a "kind of problem [that] is considered to be a form of modulation difficulty."[13]

With this review of the current views, cohesiveness, and confusion regarding sensory modulation, I now turn to explaining how these concepts are applied within this book for children.

### *The Brain Security Team*

The concept of a brain security team merges the science with the art of pediatric practice to contribute a functional explanation of the complexities of modulation in a manner that is appropriate and applicable for children. As conceptualized and presented within this book, the brain security team works to regulate both the "quantity and quality" of sensory stimuli. As the team is described as being housed within both the brain and the body, it is allowed to encompass modulatory constructs on the cellular level, including the collective activity of receptors, as well as higher-level modulatory processes such as those housed within the limbic system and salience networks. In addition, the concept of a brain security team was also crafted so that it may encompass modulation as it relates to attention and salience attribution. Language in the book describes the brain security team as able to "filter" incoming sensory information to allow it to "screen" for importance. This wording was carefully selected to reflect the science, but also to use language that is familiar and comprehensible for children. While this presentation of the information is certainly simplified for pediatric use, it does hold the overall integrity of the current research.

### *Sensory Modes*

Another broad concept presented in the book is "sensory modes." These modes are described as ways that brains can "do the same thing in different ways," alluding to the fact that when presented with the same sensory stimuli, an individual who is Sensory Over-Responsive will have a very different experience of that stimuli than someone who is Sensory Under-Responsive. The book identifies four sensory modes, delineated by the way that the brain security team is working (e.g., "Sensory Too Much" is characterized as a mode in which the security team has allowed "too much" sensory information into the brain). Surely, this is a slightly liberal application of the science, as we are not truly able to peer into a brain and determine just how much sensory information is there. However, based on observable behaviors, an understanding of modulation as a balance of excitatory and inhibitory mechanisms, and a proposed description of modulation dysfunction as too much or too little inhibition,[3] we can hypothesize about the amount and intensity of sensation reaching the brain. Using this reasoning, one would suspect that one would get *more* of excited sensory input, *less* of inhibited stimuli, and *more* of uninhibited stimuli. Again, this concept strives to bring the complexities of neuroscience into a pediatric-friendly format.

To develop these modes, I drew on the work of Miller and colleagues, who differentiate sensory modulation disorder into three subtypes labeled "Sensory Over Responsive," "Sensory Under Responsive" and "Sensory Seeking."[16] Not only do these subtypes work well to describe different states of modulatory dysfunction, they are also widely accepted and respected within the SI community. It should be noted, however, that while the classification of sensory modulation into three discrete subtypes is substantiated by research,[14,15] sensory seeking can also be viewed as a behavioral consequence of poor sensory modulation.[11] The three subtypes of sensory modulation disorder, as defined by Miller and colleagues, are delineated using behavioral outcomes, which fits their intentions of developing a diagnostic taxonomy.[16] I, in contrast, was looking for a way to explain these behaviors and symptoms to children, not to define them or apply diagnostic terms, so I turned to a categorization system that was more reflective of neural processes. Using the activity of a brain security team rather than behavior to delineate four sensory modulation subtypes was developed for the following reasons:

1. One of the main aims of this book is to translate the neuroscience of modulation into *functional knowledge* that can be *applied* to support daily activity and success. This focus on function and application necessitates a forward look to the "then what" question that comes following the exposition of knowledge. Then what does the child do with this knowledge? I find it difficult to tell a child that they are being "over-responsive" and then expect a functional outcome. How does one respond less? In what ways? And does this imply that they are doing something wrong in the way in which they respond to sensation? Or, if a child is "under responsive," how do they know and then respond more to sensory stimuli?

   In contrast, I find the functional outcome of terminology such as "too much" or "not enough" readily applicable. What does one do if they do not have enough of something? They get more. What does one do if they have too much of something? They expel or block out some of it. In regards to sensory modulation, we can easily make the jump into the "getting more" or "blocking out" sensation. In fact, these concepts align with environmental and activity modifications found in common intervention practice related to sensory modulation.[5,10,13,17] Importantly, the focus on what that reader can do *functionally* with the information is imperative to support the child's ability to manage their sensory experiences in a way that supports success.

2.  The second justification for use of modes that are delineated by neural activity rather than behavior is that it helps to reduce the stigma that may be experienced in relation to sensory modulation dysfunction. Rather than telling a child that they are "over-responsive" or "under-responsive" to sensation, which seems to allude to the fact that they are doing something wrong, the four modes presented in this book refer to how their brain security teams are operating. Thus, it provides more of a feeling that something in their body is out of calibration but can be supported, rather than that they are inherently doing or behaving in a manner that is "wrong."

Perhaps this focus on neurological processes rather than behavior is helpful as we find the words "behave" and "behavioral" used so often in appraisal of a child's actions, even when there are underlying reasons that the child may not be "behaving" per our standards. Phrases such as "behave yourself" or "be on your best behavior" suggest a certain level of control owned by the child, when in fact, we see that the original work of A. Jean Ayres was founded in looking "beyond behavior" to "gain an understanding of the neurological underpinnings of disorder."[18] In contrast, we don't typically hear phrases such as "make your brain work well" from parents or caregivers. Thus, the removal of self-stigma. I hope that this approach reflects the work of A. Jean Ayres, who devoted her professional life to understanding how sensation relates to functional behavior and how we can use those constructs to support the lives of children.

It is imperative for me to note here that the presentation of these concepts is not intended to critique the critical work of Miller and colleagues.[16] Their work has contributed so much to the field and has allowed a common language for discussing modulation disorder in clinical and diagnostic terms. I simply hope that by pointing out our different objectives, the justification of my own language will be clear.

### *Sensory Pattern Questionnaire*

The questionnaire within this book was developed to support the reader's understanding of their sensory patterns. It guides them through the process of identifying characteristic and patterned ways in which they respond to sensory stimuli, building a foundation for the management of sensory modulation challenges in daily life. While it is similar in some ways to assessments that are used in practice, it is not a clinical tool built for assessment or diagnosis; this is not the intention of the questionnaire. Acknowledgment must be given to the developers of two families of sensory-based assessments: the Sensory Processing Measure assessments and the Sensory Profile assessments, as they have brought the ability to assess sensory processing into standard clinical practice through the use of scales and questionnaires. While the questionnaire in this book was developed for different reasons and does not specifically draw upon these assessments, no sensory-based questionnaire would be complete without recognition of their work.

### *Consideration of Proprioception Regarding Modulation*

Proprioception is the only sense in this book that is not classified into all four sensory modes. This is reflective of differences in the assessment of proprioceptive found in current practice, as well as the current understanding of proprioceptive modulation. The Sensory Processing Measure 2 (SPM2) reflects differences in the assessment of proprioceptive modulation. Brief descriptions in the introduction of the manual for the SPM2 describes the scales of vision, hearing, touch, taste, smell, and balance and motion (measurement of vestibular function) as measuring over- or under-reactivity to these sensations. In contrast, the body awareness scale, a measurement of proprioception, does not include language specific to modulation.[19] Su and Parham examined the validity of sensory systems as distinct constructs and found that the vestibular and proprioceptive systems are "so strongly associated" that it might be best to assess them together as a "single functional system."[20] It should be noted, however, that this work was not specific to modulation. Lane notes that "poor proprioceptive modulation has been less well defined but some research supports proprioceptive seeking as a possible modulation concern."[3] In fact, the schematic representation of sensory integrative dysfunction developed and used throughout *Sensory Integration Theory and Practice, 3rd Edition* does not have an arrow from proprioception pointing left toward the side of the schematic that indicates modulation dysfunction. That being said, the text clearly states that sensory modulation dysfunction (over- and under-responsivity) can be seen in any sensory system,[11] and Lane, Lynn, and Reynolds specifically state that sensory over-responsivity "can occur in any sensory system."[5]

And finally, I must express sincere and deep gratitude for the researchers, clinicians, and educators who have worked to provide an understanding of sensory modulation. Your commitment, dedication, and endless hours have changed countless lives. This book would not be possible without your work.

"If I have seen further, it is by standing on the shoulders of giants."

— Isaac Newton

# Acknowledgments

I have heard that it takes a village to raise a child, but it seems it also takes a village to publish a book. This book would not be possible without the help and support of so many people, whom I would like to thank.

Thank you to the incredible team of scientists who have committed so much time and effort into researching and making sense of sensory processing and integration. This book stands on the work that you have done. You cannot imagine how many children, families, and individuals have benefitted from your unwavering commitment to investigate the complexities of how humans take in sensory information and use it to shape their lives. I have spent countless hours reviewing your work and made every attempt to stay true to the science that you have developed.

Thank you to my colleagues who have worked alongside me, sharing knowledge and wisdom, encouraging me along the way, answering millions of questions, and inspiring me with your work. The world (and most certainly my world!) is better because of you.

Thank you to the incredible faculty, both past and present, of Virginia Commonwealth University. There is no way to express my full gratitude and admiration for your dedication to the field of occupational therapy and to the education of its students. I cannot imagine a better place to start a career. If you consider all of the students whom you have inspired, all of the clients that they go on to treat, those client's families and the people that they, in turn, impact through their well-being and daily occupations, it is simply incomprehensible to quantify or qualify the positive contributions that you have made to the world.

Dr. Carole Ivey, you have been a mentor from the beginning of my OT journey. Thank you for every conversation. You always leave me with clarity and more thinking to do.

Dr. Tony Gentry, when I had no idea what my next move for publishing a book should be, you had the exact guidance that I needed. Thank you for your support and for helping me to widen my vision.

Abby Finkelstein, your understanding of the brain and how it contributes to the human experience is immense. Your knowledge and leading questions undoubtedly made this book better. I cannot thank you enough. The field of OT is going to benefit greatly from your work.

Thank you to my dear friend and colleague, Paige Hebard, who listened when this program was simply an idea, read through never-ending versions, guided the content, asked pertinent questions, edited and edited, and, most of all, always believed.

Thank you to Hannah Newlon and Marika Emanuel Smith for taking the time to review the manuscript and offer such valuable input from a clinical perspective. The book is undoubtedly better because of your efforts.

Dawn and Steve Lewellyn, your capacity to be always ready with whatever support is needed is unmatched. Thank you for supporting this book, my career, and countless kids and families along the way. I am so thankful that our paths crossed.

Justin, you have been there through my entire OT journey, including the development of this book. You have listened to more of my ideas than I care to admit. Thanks for encouraging me to chase this one.

Thank you to my sisters, my best friends, who have read and re-read, listened and re-listened, and always, always encouraged. You two are the best.

Thank you to Regina for always having and sharing faith.

Thank you to my parents who have invested so much, starting from the time when I was little but had big ideas. I am so thankful that, at least for a short time, we have been right down the road from you.

Mackenzie, you are the joy of my life and my best and most favorite thing. Thank you for keeping me focused on what is important in life. When you made us a family, you helped me see my work from a different viewpoint and made me want to work even harder.

And thank you to the Maker of all good things for letting me put down in words some ideas that I hope will help the people living in Your world. The brain is truly a magnificent creation.

# Introduction to Being a Brain Executive

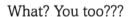

Okay, I could be wrong here, but I feel like everyone is talking about sensory this and sensory that and sensory processing and sensory integration and sensory breaks and sensory exercises and *sensory whatever* and I feel like it has something to do with me, but here's the problem, I HAVE NO IDEA WHAT IT'S ALL ABOUT.

What? You too???

*Oh, and "Hi!"*

## Welcome

Welcome to the Brain Executive program, where you can learn about how your brain works and how to help it work a little better. What does this have to do with sensory *whatevers*? Everything, because sensory processing (you'll learn more about exactly what that is later) happens in the brain. As a Brain Executive, you can actually learn to manage your brain to help it work better. Pretty awesome, right? And the best part is, helping your brain helps you to do things that you want and need to do, and to do them better—like school stuff, which is important and all, but also things like playing sports or gaming or hanging out with your friends.

Well, I didn't say *the ultimate gamer* … but yeah, you can totally get better at doing whatever is important to you. If that's gaming, well, you do you.

Ready to get started? Or at least want to learn a little more? Let's begin with some basics about the brain and being a Brain Executive.

## Brain Executive – The Brain Part

I am guessing that you already know that you have a brain. But do you know what your brain actually does? Sure, it does the obvious stuff like thinking and learning, but that's just part of it. Your brain is basically the command center for your whole body and is responsible for things like how you think, feel, and act. In fact, almost everything you do involves your brain in some way. Want some examples? You got it.

For starters, your brain takes in a ton of information from the world around you and makes sense out of it. Did you know that you have a spot in your brain just for figuring out what you see? You also have a place in your brain just for your sense of touch—you know, so you can feel when somebody taps you on the shoulder or what it feels like to touch a snake (kinda *ewww*, but surprisingly not at all slimy). You even have areas that are specially designed for hearing and places in your brain where smelly feet are smelled. All of this has a lot to do with sensory *whatevers*.

But that's not all your brain does. Your brain also tells your body how and when to move—raise your right hand, wiggle your big toe, nod your head, get up and run, now walk. All of that happens with commands from your brain.

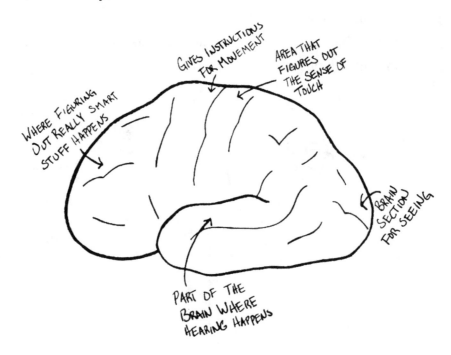

Also, I hate to break it to you, but feeling sad or happy or in love doesn't actually happen in your heart. That thing is just for pumping blood around and stuff. It's your *brain* that does all of that feelings stuff!

And don't forget the thinking and learning part, because your brain does that too, and it is one of the most complex things that it does. Our incredible ability to think like the smartie humans that we are is what sets us apart from other animals. For example, a smart dog knows how to sit, come when you whistle, lie down, and maybe roll over or play dead. A smart human can do stuff like build a rocket and go to the moon.

## Workbook Section: Brain Exec Activity – The Brain

Did you know that your brain does so much? We don't think about it most of the time, but our brains are always working. Take a minute and think about all that your brain has been doing since you sat down to read. Can you write down some of what it has been doing below?

What have you seen, heard, smelled, tasted, or felt?

What body parts have moved?

Have you felt any emotions?

What have you learned?

# Brain Executive – The Executive Part

What's an executive? An executive is basically a boss. It's the person who tells everybody what to do (and then the people actually do it … unlike when my older sister tries to tell me what to do and I just ignore her). You've heard of a CEO of a business, right? CEO stands for Chief Executive Officer. It's the person who is in charge and runs the whole company. The CEO is an expert about the company and manages it so that everyone is doing their best work and making the business the best that it can be. Without the CEO being in charge, everyone would be doing whatever they want and would probably do the wrong things at the wrong time or do too much or too little and in general just not work together well. So the whole executive thing is pretty important—they tell everyone what to do so that the whole company does its best work.

# Brain Executive – Putting It Together

Now you might be thinking, *That's great, but I don't own a company.* True, BUT YOU DO OWN A BRAIN. Which means you can be a BEO, or a Brain Executive Officer—a person who is the boss of their brain so that it does its best work. Just like a CEO is in charge of a company, a BEO is in charge of a brain. Wait, *what?!* I can tell my brain what to do? Well, not exactly just tell it what to do, but you can definitely manage it so that it does more of the right things and less of the not-so-right things. It's like this: you can't just say "Brain, do this," or "Brain, do that" and boss it around all day. But you can learn to talk and listen to your brain in a way that helps it be its best. And helping our brains be their best is what we are going for here, Exec.

> A **Brain Exec** *is a person who is the boss of their brain!*

Anyway, the brain sort of has its own language, and to be a good boss you have to know how to speak it. Think of it as learning "Brain Language," which is kind of like sign language because your brain understands things that you *do* more than when you just try to yell directions at it. Plus, it's not all about telling your brain what to do. To be a good boss, you also have to *listen*. Yeah, that's right; you have to listen to your brain and maybe even ask it a few questions like "Hey, how are you doing up there?" and "Do you need a little help?" When you learn how your brain is working, you can help it work better by changing some of the things that you do and when you do them.

# Introduction to Being a Brain Executive

☑ **Brain Fact:** *You can communicate with your brain by the things that you do!*

People are usually surprised when they learn they can be the boss of their brain, but if your brain is so important and the command center for your whole body, shouldn't you be in charge of it? I mean, otherwise you are just letting it run around and do whatever it wants. Imagine a preschool class without a teacher. Agh! Brains on the loose! But this is your brain, which (don't forget!) controls pretty much everything you do. So, if it's wild chaos in there with no one in charge, well, it might make it hard to do some of the things that you need to do if your command center is chaos, Exec.

Okay, so maybe that's a little dramatic. But here is the thing: your brain does a bunch of stuff that you aren't even aware of—some of it good, some not so helpful. A big part of what we will learn to do is figure out exactly how your brain is working and help it work a little better. And where does the sensory *whatever* come in? Well, we have to figure out exactly what that stuff is and how it is working in your brain, how it is helping you out, and how we can help it out some too.

This is where being a Brain Executive comes in. Being the boss of your brain means understanding what is going on in there, managing it, and sometimes adjusting it. Pretty amazing, right? Now, back up for a sec and read that sentence again that starts "Being the boss of your brain means ..." See the middle part? The one that says you have to understand what is happening in your brain? That is what a lot of becoming a Brain Executive is going to be about: learning about your brain. I mean, an executive can't exactly run a company that they don't know anything about. What if the CEO of a pizza company didn't know what pizza should taste like? Or the CEO of a car company didn't know how to drive? Probably not the best choice for a boss. Well then, hello, if you are the **B**EO of your brain, you should probably know what's going on up there in your head!

Sensory 101

# So, What is All This Sensory Stuff About?

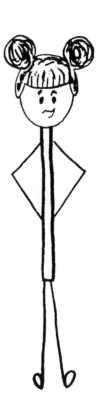

Definitely time that we talk about all this sensory stuff, since that is sort of why you're reading all of this anyway. Okay, here it goes. You know about your five senses, right? The senses of sight, smell, touch, taste, and hearing. These are basically the way that your body gets information from the world around you. Like, oh, I see a super cute puppy over there and I think I am going to go hug him. Or, what is that amazing smell? It's pizza and I want to eat some right now! And oh my gosh that pizza tastes so good. Or I hear my favorite song playing—turn it up! Or what do I feel on my arm?! Is it a spider crawling on me?!?!?! Ahhhhhhh!!!!! All of the things that you see, smell, taste, hear or feel are things in the world around you that you know are there because of your eyes, ears, nose, taste buds, and skin.

Pause and let's do a word game here. What does the word "sense" remind you of that we have been talking about? Sensory, right? Yeah, all this sensory *whatever* has to do with your senses and how you take in and use information from the world around you.

# Workbook Section: Brain Exec Activity – KWL Chart

Before we jump in, we are going to do a little activity to prep your mind for what we are about to learn. It's called a KWL Chart. Peek two pages ahead and you will see a big rectangle that's divided into three parts. This is your KWL chart to fill out. In the first part you are going to write everything that you already **K**now about sensory *whatever*. This is just a brain dump, so write anything that you can think of that you know. In the second part you are going to write down anything that you **W**ant to know about sensory *whatever*. Think about any questions that you have and write them here. The last part you actually don't fill out yet. It is for writing everything that you **L**earned about sensory *whatever*, and you will fill this out at the end of the book. Check out the next page for an example KWL Chart.

| What I <u>K</u>now Already | What I <u>W</u>ant to Know | What I <u>L</u>earned |
|---|---|---|
| Brainstorm about everything that you already know about sensory stuff and write it down here. Don't even worry about if it is true or not; we can fact check later!<br><br>*Examples:* We take "Sensory Breaks" in class when we need to move. There is a "Sensory Room" at school. The 5 senses are sight, hearing, touch, smell, and taste | Here you are going to write down anything that you want to know about sensory stuff. Think of any questions that you have or what you might be wondering about.<br><br>*Examples:* Why is everyone talking about sensory stuff so much? How does moving around in a "Sensory Break" help you learn? What exactly goes on in the Sensory Room? | Leave this blank! At the end of the book we will come back and fill this one in. |
| What I <u>K</u>now Already | What I <u>W</u>ant to Know | What I <u>L</u>earned |
|  |  |  |

# The Five Senses

Let's do a quick review of the five senses, because don't forget that a Brain Executive wants to know exactly what is going on in their brain, which means we need to make sure that we know exactly what is going on with our senses.

### Sight

The sense of sight allows us to see. It tells us about light in our environment and the color, shape, and size of things around us. It even tells us how something is moving, like when you see a car driving down the road and you can tell that it is moving instead of sitting still and which way it is going. Oh, and sight lets us know how one object relates to another, like how you can tell that the socks are on the chair next to the lamp because you can see all three things at the same time. Hey, get your dirty socks off my chair!!!

### Hearing

The sense of hearing allows us to detect sounds in our environment and gives us information about what caused the sound, how loud the sound is, and if it is high-pitched like the squeak of a mouse or low-pitched like thunder. Hearing also gives us the ability to distinguish specific sounds, like when we listen to someone talking. The ability to hear the difference between the sounds "snah" and "cah" make it possible to hear the difference between the words "snake" and "cake" when

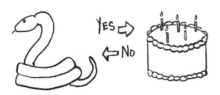

someone says them. Which is super important because I don't know about you, but I totally want to eat a piece of cake and definitely *do not* want to eat a piece of snake. No. Thank. You.

### Taste

The sense of taste tells us about what you have in your mouth and if you like it or not. Like, wow, I love these cookies, but eww, those brussels sprouts taste gross. Hopefully it's food you're tasting, but let's be honest: even if it isn't food, you can still taste it. When you were a toddler, you probably chewed on crayons or blocks. And guess what? They have a taste to them. Tell me I'm wrong. Anyway … taste can tell us whether we want to eat what is in our mouth and even whether it's safe to eat.

### *Smell*

The sense of smell allows us to, well, smell what's around us. A lot of things give off tiny chemicals into the air called odorants, and when those little chemicals floating around in the air get to our nose, we can smell them. Some things, like flowers, give off good-smelling chemicals, but others, like skunks, give off pretty bad-smelling chemicals. Also, farts. Farts smell bad. (Sorry, had to get that out there.) The sense of smell can help inform us about if we like something or if we should avoid something.

Pro tip: *avoid people who are farting.*

### *Touch*

The sense of touch tells us when something contacts our skin. It also gives us information about exactly what is touching our skin, how much and how hard it is touching our skin, and whether it is moving. Think about it: with your eyes closed, you could totally tell the difference between a ball hitting you in the arm and a bug crawling up your arm. That's your sense of touch. Humans have an extra-sensitive sense of touch on their hands and face. In fact, this super-sensitive touch in our hands is one reason why humans can do things like write with a pen or zip a zipper. What's that? Oh yeah, it also helps you play video games.

# Workbook Section:
# Brain Exec Activity – The 5 Senses

How are your five senses working? In the boxes below, write down everything that your senses are taking in right now. How much are you seeing, hearing, tasting, smelling, and touching? Are some of your senses detecting more than others?

Sight

Hearing

Taste

Smell

Touch

# But Wait, That's Not All

Prepare yourself, because I am about to blow your mind. [dramatic pause] You actually have more than just the five senses you learned about in school. Wait, whaaaatttttt????? Yeah, it's totally true. There are two more senses that you need to know about. They are sort of invisible senses, so maybe that is why they don't teach them in first grade. I don't know; you'll have to go ask your first-grade teacher. But you definitely have two more, and here they are.

### *Proprioception*

Proprioception is the sense that tells you about where your body parts are and how they move. You have little detectors in your joints that can tell when they bend or move. You also have detectors in your muscles that can tell when the muscle moves and how tense it is. Proprioception even tells your brain how fast and which way your body parts are moving. Anytime your muscles or joints move or your muscles tense up, these tiny detectors shout up to your brain to let it know.[21,22]

*HEY BRAIN, ITS MOVING!*

# Workbook Section: Brainy Experiment

Try this: close your eyes, and then raise your arm above your head. Can you tell whether it is moving without looking at it? That's your proprioceptive system. Okay, next, try this. Close your eyes and then squeeze all your muscles really tightly. Can you feel when they tighten up? That's your proprioceptive system too.

Why is this important? Good question! Proprioception lets you know what your body is doing without having to look at it. Has this ever happened to you? You are walking along, talking to a friend, and all of a sudden you step on something like a rock or the edge of a sidewalk that makes your foot turn sideways. You almost fall, but your super-stealthy skills save you at the last minute. Phew. So that moment when your foot turned sideways—it made your ankle bend and caused some of the muscles on the side of your foot and leg to stretch. Your proprioceptive detectors in the joint and muscles are why you could sense that happening without looking.

If you haven't noticed yet, I love experiments. They really help you understand the science we are talking about, plus they are fun. Here's another, and for this one you need a snack to eat. (If whoever is in charge said no snacks before dinner, tell them sorry, this is for SCIENCE. If they don't go for it, just pretend you have a snack.)

*EXPERIMENTS ARE AWESOME, PLUS THEY HELP YOU LEARN!*

# Workbook Section:
# Brainy Experiment

Here's what you do: pick up a piece of the snack, bring it to your mouth, and eat it. Taaa-dahhhhhh! What? You're not impressed? Okay, but now, pick up a piece of the snack and then *close your eyes*, bring it to your mouth and eat it. Hey! How did you know where your mouth was and how did you bring your hand right to it without looking? Proprioception, my friend! Those little detectors told your brain exactly where your arm and hand and mouth are and how to move. And really, think about it. How often are you paying attention to how to get food to your mouth? Basically never. You are busy talking to a friend or watching TV, and your proprioceptive system just takes over and helps out because that's what it's for. Pretty cool, right?

Anyone out there miss your mouth when your eyes were closed? That's okay, it just might mean that your proprioceptive system needs a little help from your eyes. Don't forget: we are here to learn about your brain—what it does super great and what it needs a little help on.

 **Brain Fact:** *Proprioception is the sense that tells you about where your body parts are, how they are moving, and how tense your muscles are.*

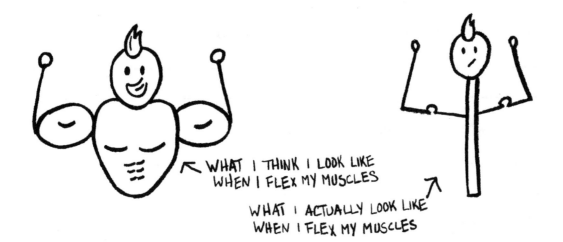

WHAT I THINK I LOOK LIKE WHEN I FLEX MY MUSCLES

WHAT I ACTUALLY LOOK LIKE WHEN I FLEX MY MUSCLES

# Workbook Section:
# Brain Exec Activity – Proprioception

Ready to test out your proprioceptive system a little more? Grab someone nearby, because you need a helper. For this experiment you are going to close your eyes and start moving your body. Maybe raise your arms above your head, maybe cross your legs, maybe sit down and then stand up, use your imagination.

Before we really get going, though, test out how moving with your eyes closed feels and take it slow at first. If you don't feel steady with your eyes closed, you can totally do this while you are sitting or even lying down.

Okay, got a feel for it? Now you are going to start moving your body with your eyes closed, and at some point your helper is going to say "Freeze!" When this happens, your job is to stop moving your body and freeze in place ... but don't open your eyes! Now, with your eyes closed can you describe how your body is positioned? Is your arm above your head? Both or just one? Is your head turned to the right or left? What parts of your body are touching the ground? Yell out what you think your body is doing, and your helper can check for you. Now repeat this a few times to really put your proprioceptive system to the test, and then answer a few questions.

How did it feel to move your body with your eyes closed?

_____

_____

Could you tell where all your body parts were without looking?

_____

_____

Was it easier to tell where your arms or legs were?

_____

_____

Could you tell the difference between your right and left sides?

_____

_____

### Vestibular

If you thought proprioception was weird, wait for this one. The vestibular system is a set of tubes and sacs way down deep inside your ear that tell you about how your head is positioned and moving.[21,22] I know, right? This is basically like alien stuff. Except it's not, because actually all humans have this. What? Do aliens have this too? I have no idea, but the next time I meet up with one I'll ask for you. (That was sarcastic, by the way, because do you think I actually meet up with aliens?) Back to the vestibular system.

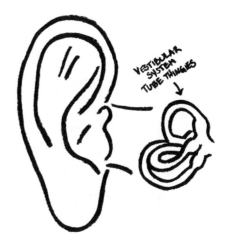

So, no joke, way deep inside your ears you have this set of tube-loop-sac thingies. The sides of these tubes and sacs are lined with tiny little hairs, and the tube/sac thingies are filled with fluid. When you move your head, the fluid moves, which bends the little hairs, and when the little hairs bend, a signal is sent to your brain telling it "Hey! Your head is moving!" It even tells it about how it is moving, like left, right, spinning, shaking, fast, slow, and stuff like that. And that isn't all. These hairs can detect the positions of your head, like right-side-up, upside-down, or sideways.[21,22]

So, this works when you do things like shake your head "yes" or "no," but it also works when your whole body moves because (*surprise!*) your head is attached to your body. Actions like jumping, spinning, and swinging all move your head around and make your vestibular system signal to your brain that you are moving. So do things like turning upside down. In fact, humans don't turn upside down that much, so doing that sends mega-signals to your brain. And regular movements such as standing up, walking, turning, and stopping all move the fluid in the tube-thingies and activate your vestibular system. What was that? Rollercoasters? Oh yeah, those make your vestibular system go wild!

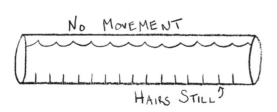

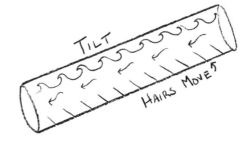

# Workbook Section:
# Brain Exec Activity – Vestibular

Let's take a look at exactly how these tube/sac thingies of your vestibular system work. No, we aren't going to actually look inside your ear. I have a really great way to show you how moving your head affects the vestibular system without doing major surgery. (You can thank me later.) For this you will need a clear water bottle that has a top and a large mirror, like a bathroom mirror, that you can stand in front of. Fill the bottle about ¾ of the way with water and then screw the lid on tight. Okay, now stand in front of the mirror and hold the water bottle up against the side of your head, next to your ear. Now, make a movement that moves your head. Maybe do a side bend or nod your head yes or shake your head no. Did the water in the bottle move? That is *exactly* how your vestibular system works! Every time your head moves, the fluid moves inside the tube/sac thingies, sending a signal to your brain that says "Hey! Your head is moving!" Okay, now let's try some different kinds of movement. How about jumping around or spinning? How else can you make the water in the bottle move?

Below, brainstorm a list of movements that you make every day that "move the water" in your vestibular system. Can you come up with at least 10?

_____

_____

_____

_____

_____

_____

_____

_____

_____

_____

# Workbook Section:
# Brain Dump

Is your brain exploding with all of this new knowledge?! Take a minute and write down all the new stuff that you just learned about your brain and sensory systems.

_____

_____

_____

_____

_____

_____

_____

_____

_____

_____

### *Okay, So Exactly What is the Brain Doing in All This?*

This sensory *whatever* is starting to come together. We've covered all the stuff that is happening in your skin, ears, eyes, nose, mouth, joints, and muscles. And we even said that all the information gathered from these places is sent to the brain. What exactly happens after that? Does the brain just gather all the information up like a big book that has a ton of information stored in it? Nope. The brain is way more interesting than that. Your brain takes all that information in, makes sense out of it, and then decides what to do about it.[23]

Brain Fact: *Your brain takes in sensory information, makes sense out of it, and then decides what to do about it.*

Let's take your sense of sight for instance. Did you know that if your eyes weren't connected to your brain, you wouldn't be able to see? I'm for real. There is a special kind of blindness called "cortical blindness" where your eyes work just fine but the brain doesn't, so the person can't see.[24] I am telling you: your brain is a super important part of all this sensory stuff.

Also, don't forget that the brain *makes sense* of all this information,[21] so even if you maybe see something, you don't really know what it is or what it means without your brain.[25] Take a baby, for instance, whose brain hasn't learned anything yet about what they are seeing. Show a baby a snake and their eyes will see it, but their brain won't know what it is. So the baby picks the snake up and starts playing with it like a string. Yikes! *Your* brain, on the other hand, knows something about snakes and what they are, so if you see one, you are probably going to avoid it. How? Your brain takes in information from your eyes, identifies that shape as a snake, and then says, "Hey, that thing might bite, better stay away."

And that whole process when your senses detect something and send the info to your brain, which does some smart thinking and knows how to respond … that is called "sensory processing" or "sensory integration."

# Sensory Processing and What It's All About

This whole sensory processing/integration idea is pretty important, so let's unpack it a little more. Decoding the separate words "sensory," "processing," and "integration" is a good place to start.

### *Sensory*

We've already talked about this one a lot, so just a quick review here. Sensory is about how your body takes in information with your senses to inform your brain about what is going on in the environment around you (what you see, hear, taste, smell, and feel) and what is going on inside you (how your body feels and is moving and positioned).

### *Processing*

To process something means to go through a series of steps so that what you started with, in sort of a basic form, changes to become a finished product. For example, you can think of cooking breakfast as a process. You combine some raw eggs, butter, and milk, put them in a pan, and turn on the stove. Then you cook and stir them for a few minutes, and finally, at the end of this *process*, you have scrambled eggs. Voila! You followed some steps and changed raw eggs and milk into something yummy and edible.

Your brain does something sort of similar when it processes sensory information. It takes "raw" information coming in from your eyes, ears, nose, mouth, skin, and joints and puts it through some steps to make a finished product that your brain can use. Let's think more in-depth about that example of seeing a snake. First, the detectors in your eyes see the shape and colors of something on the ground. Then, those detectors send that information all the way to your brain. Next, your brain registers that info, organizes it, and accesses stored knowledge about things that have that shape. Say it comes up with two things that are long, skinny, brown-colored, and found on the ground—snakes and sticks. Your brain then analyzes what it sees a bit more and decides that since the object is moving and has eyes, it must be a snake. And then

your brain does this really awesome thing. It goes, "Okay, that is a snake, and snakes can be venomous. I'd better make my body move out of the way," and it sends signals out to your legs to make you move. Quickly, please!

Wow, that is a lot of stuff for your brain to do just to figure out something pretty simple. And all those

steps to go from raw info (it's a long, skinny, brown-colored object on the ground) to a finished product (that's a snake and I should get away!)—that is a process. And guess what? Since it is a process that uses your senses, we call it "Sensory Processing."

### *Integration*

Integration means to combine things in a way that is meaningful. What do I mean by meaningful? Here's an example: say you decide to make someone a bracelet. (Your grandmother? A friend? Your cat, to wear as a collar? I don't know; you have to figure out who you are giving this imaginary bracelet to.) So you take some string and some beads and put them in a box, shake them all around, and give them as a gift. Wait a second, you just gave someone a box with some string and beads in it. What are they supposed to do with that? Nothing. Okay, but say that instead, you take the string and beads and *put them together in a meaningful way*. (Ummm, integrate them? Yes!) So you organize the colors of the beads, put them on the string one at a time in a certain order, tie the string up with a good knot, and BOOM: you made a really great accessory to wear.

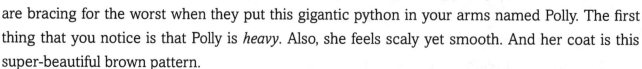

Your brain does this with sensory info. I mean, putting things together in a meaningful way, not making a bracelet. Instead of using string and beads, it takes sensory information from your environment around you and from what's going on inside your body and integrates them with each other and with knowledge stored in your brain.[7,11,21,25]

Let's put a slight twist on the snake scenario and use it to understand sensory integration. Say this time you are on a field trip to a zoo and you are chosen to be the kid who gets to hold a snake. (Technically, you are the second kid chosen, but the first one was too scared. You are sort of scared too, but you are acting like you aren't because, hello, everyone is watching.) So you are bracing for the worst when they put this gigantic python in your arms named Polly. The first thing that you notice is that Polly is *heavy*. Also, she feels scaly yet smooth. And her coat is this super-beautiful brown pattern.

Pause here, because you just *integrated* three different senses. Your vision told you about Polly's color and coat pattern, your sense of touch told you about how smooth her scales feel, and it was actually your sense of proprioception that told you about how heavy she is. How? When the weight of Polly made your arms move down a little and made your muscles work harder to hold her up, well, your sense of proprioception is what detected all of that. This information was put together in a meaningful way to tell your brain about Polly. What's next? More integration!

About this time, Polly starts moving around in your arms. It turns out that you must be a snake charmer because Polly really likes you! She even tries to give you a big hug. Awwwww, Polly, you're the best. I like you too, Pal. (Note here, Exec: It's your sense of touch that can feel Polly moving and squeezing you!)

But wait, the snake-keeper's eyes are getting big and she starts to move fast toward you. What's wrong???

At this moment your brain kicks into integration overdrive. It accesses a bunch of stored information about snakes and adds it together with what you are feeling. The next few seconds go something like this:

*Pythons circle and squeeze their prey just before eating them.*
*The snake-keeper is running toward you, looking terrified.*
*Polly is circling your body and starting to tighten up.*
*OMG. Does Polly want to eat me?!?!?!*

Thank goodness your brain integrated stored knowledge, the feeling of Polly, and the look of the snake-keeper so fast! You quickly start trying to get Polly off of you, and the snake-keeper grabs her just in time. Phew! That was a close one. Thank. You. Brain.

# Workbook Section:
# Brain Exec Activity – Processing and Integration

Making a bracelet out of beads and a string was an example of putting things together in a meaningful way. You could also say it's a *process* to string all the beads together and make a finished product. Can you think of other examples of processes or ways to integrate pieces to make something meaningful?

_____

_____

_____

_____

_____

Making a mosaic is another great example of putting different pieces together to make something meaningful. Get a few different colors or paper and tear them into small pieces. Then arrange the pieces (and glue them down if you want!) to make a work of art. Could you call putting all the tiny pieces of paper together in a meaningful way integration? You bet!

# That's Kind of Awesome, But Why Is It So Important?

I mentioned before that being a Brain Executive means knowing amazing things about your brain, right? I mean, there are things happening in there all the time that most people don't even know about! But knowing incredible brain facts is only part of being a Brain Exec. What's more important are these questions: #1. How does all this help you in your everyday life? #2. When what's going on inside your brain is not working super well, how can we help it? So let's take a look at why all of this sensory stuff is important to answer that first question. The answer to Question #2 will come a little later in the book.

Again, all of this sensory information works to tell your brain about what is going on around you (what you see and hear and all) and what is going on inside you (how your body is moving and feeling). Because the things that you do every day involves these senses, sensory processing and integration have a huge impact on your daily life. Things like moving, learning, communicating, making friends, and being social are all affected by sensory processing.[23,26]

Let's take a closer look at this idea, Exec.

## Opportunities and What to Avoid

For one, what you notice around you in your environment helps you to know what opportunities there are.[26] If you didn't know there was music playing, how could you show off your epic dance moves? If you didn't notice that delish smell, how could you know to show up to dinner because, pizza! If your sense of touch wasn't working, how could you know how great it feels to pet your dog's ears? So, sensory processing and integration helps you to know all of the amazing things you could be doing. Which is good, because you only live once!

On the other hand, noticing stuff around you also helps you know what to avoid.[26] Like, thanks, but on second thought, I'll pass on that pizza because there are anchovies on it and I don't eat tiny little smelly fish with their eyes looking at me. Eww. Or nope, I'm not riding in the back seat of your car because I get carsick and I might vomit. Or, well, do I have to bring up avoiding people who are farting again?

So you see, your ability to process and integrate all the stuff your senses are detecting helps you to know what you want to do and what you don't want to do. Without it you could miss out on some great stuff and you could get stuck doing some not-so-great stuff.

## Workbook Section:
## Brain Exec Activity – Opportunities and What to Avoid

Think of something that you like to do and something that you do not like to do and then describe how your senses make you feel about them. For instance, I like pepperoni pizza because of how it tastes and smells, but I do not want to eat sardine pizza because it smells like old fish, it's gross, and I don't like the way the fish's eyes look.

| LIKE | DON'T LIKE |
| --- | --- |
| _____ | _____ |
| _____ | _____ |
| _____ | _____ |
| _____ | _____ |

## Alertness and Arousal (AKA How Awake You Feel)

Have you ever felt so bored that you could barely stay awake? Or so excited that you feel like you just had ten energy drinks and you want to run around everywhere and do everything all at once? Or maybe like you were paying super-attention to something and were crushing it because of your stellar focus? Guess what? This all has to do with sensory processing! I am not even kidding. Let me explain …

**Brain Fact:** *All of the sensory information that your brain gets and processes affects how awake and alert you feel.*

We learned earlier that when your senses are activated (like when you feel or hear something), that information travels from your hands or ears or wherever up to your brain. Just before it gets to your brain, it goes through this little thing called the brainstem. The brainstem is sort of like the stem of a flower, but instead of hold-

BRAINSTEM
( WHERE RAS
IS LOCATED )

FLOWERSTEM

ing up a flower, it holds up your brain. Unless, of course, you have flowers for brains. And in that case, I really can't help you and maybe you are reading the wrong book. Anyway, in this brainstem thing, there is a place called the Reticular Activating System, or "RAS" for short. When sensory information gets to the RAS, the RAS's job is to tell the brain to wake up and get ready because something is happening and it needs to pay attention.[3,5,9] Think of it like when your brother yells upstairs to you that everyone is leaving in ten minutes to see a movie so you'd better get ready.

HEY BRAIN,
BE ALERT AND
GET READY!

RAS

Basically, when sensory information comes in (like when you move or see or hear or touch something), the RAS tells your brain to wake up and pay attention. When this is working just right, you feel awake and alert and you pay attention to the important stuff that is going on. Like maybe you are doing a science experiment, totally focused on what is happening, feeling perfectly alert and paying attention, because, hey, *is this thing going to blow?!* On the other hand, if there isn't a lot going on around you and you aren't moving (think boring class and you are stuck at your desk), your RAS stops telling your brain to wake up, so your brain starts to get tired and drowsy. In contrast, if there is a ton of stuff going on around you (for instance, at an amusement park with people moving around everywhere, lots to look at, everyone is talking, and the rides are making loud noises), your RAS keeps telling your brain to wake up, wake up, wake up, wake up,

SENSORY
INPUT → RAS

BE ALERT,
SOMETHING
IS HAPPENING

NO
SENSORY
INPUT -X-> RAS

CHILL & REST
NOTHING
IS GOING ON

wake up, and before you know it, your brain is like "I AM SO AWAKE" and that's when you feel like you've had ten energy drinks.[3]

So sensory input helps us know when to be awake and alert so that we can pay attention, focus, and participate when we need to. Spoiler alert: When the RAS isn't doing its job quite right, we can feel bored or tired or wildly awake at the wrong times. We will talk more about this soon to help figure out what exactly is going on in the brain at times like this and learn things we can do to help our brain be the right amount of awake.

# Workbook Section:
# Brain Exec Activity – Alertness and Arousal

Can you think of a time you were so bored that you could barely stay awake? Write about what was happening and how you felt.

_____

_____

_____

_____

_____

Can you think of a time when you felt really alert and awake? Sometimes this happens when we are excited about something, but can you think of a time when it was because there was a lot going on around you? Write about what was happening and how you felt.

_____

_____

_____

_____

_____

# Learning and Doing Things

How awake and alert you feel affects how you learn and do things.[3] Think about it. How easy is it to learn algebra when you are basically falling asleep in your chair? How easy is it to listen to directions from a grown-up when you are so excited to be at the amusement park that you just want to run around and start riding all the rides twice? (Ummm, where did you say to meet back up again?) It turns out that being the right amount of awake and alert is pretty important for learning and doing most things, and we just learned how your amount of awake/alert is connected to your sensory processing system.

Your sensory system also helps you focus on *whatever* is important for what you are doing.[3,5,7] We are going to learn way more about this soon because it is super important, but here's a preview. There is always a lot going on around and inside you, and you can't possibly pay attention to all of it at once, so your brain filters some of it out. For instance, there are about 400 words on this page, but you are really only paying attention to a few of them at a time so that you can read. I mean, do you know what the third word on the top row is? (Okay, well, after I said that, you totally looked and now you do, but before you looked you had no idea, right?) Anyway, if your brain didn't do this focus thing, it would be hard to learn or do anything. Like when you are trying to pay attention in class but you keep getting distracted by things to look at or things that you hear, and before you know it the class is over and you didn't learn a thing. Or what about when you are trying to watch your fave TV show and your little sister keeps talking? (Shhhhhhhhhh, I can't concentrate and I need to know what happens!) So yeah, sensory processing has a *huge* impact on learning and doing things because it influences how awake and alert you are and your ability to focus and pay attention, all of which are mega-important.

But that isn't all! Don't forget the simple ways that sensory input influences your learning and doing. During geography class, can you see the map and read all of the places listed on it? Thanks, visual sensory system! During basketball practice, can you hear your coach tell you to keep your eye on the net? Thanks, hearing sensory system! Sensory input has a major impact on how you learn and do things.[11]

# Workbook Section:
# Brain Exec Activity – Learning and Doing Thing

Can you describe how it feels to be alert and focused while you are learning or doing something with attention?

_____

_____

_____

_____

_____

_____

_____

Tell about a time when this was working well. What were you learning or doing? How did it feel?

_____

_____

_____

_____

_____

_____

_____

_____

Tell about a time when this was not working so well. What were you trying to learn or do? How did it feel?

_____

_____

_____

_____

_____

_____

_____

_____

# How You Act and Make Choices

But wait, there's more! When you start putting all this together, it turns out that sensory processing even plays a role in how you act and what choices you make.[3,11,26] It sounds complicated, but if you toss all this around in your mind for a sec, it turns out to be true. Think about how kids act in the library versus how kids act at recess. In the library, everything is quiet and no one moves around a whole lot, so all this goes into the brain and the brain says, "Looks like I'd better be calm, talk quietly, and not run around." On the other hand, at recess everything is loud and people are running all over, so the brain says, "Looks like everybody is running around all wild and being loud, so I guess I will join in." (If you are sitting there thinking, "Wait a sec, I don't like to run around at recess or I always get in trouble for talking too loud in the library," just hang on, because we are going to learn how different brains work differently soon. But in general, it's true

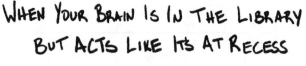

WHEN YOUR BRAIN IS IN THE LIBRARY BUT ACTS LIKE IT'S AT RECESS

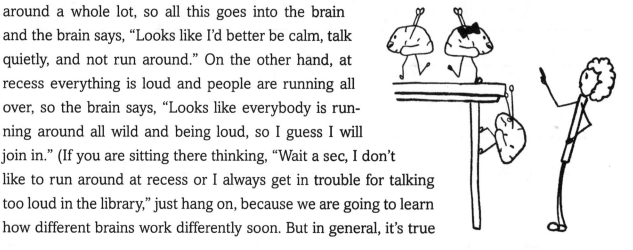

that people are quiet and calm in the library and loud and active at recess, and this all has to do with sensory processing.)

You also make a lot of choices based on your sensory processing system.[3,26] For instance, if you are a person who really hates loud noise, you might skip out on the school dance because between the music playing and everyone talking … no thanks. But if you are a person who really likes noise, you might choose to have the TV playing in the background plus music on, all while you are trying to do homework. Some people call it distracting, you call it your sweet spot.

And don't forget the whole alertness-and-arousal thing. How awake, alert, overwhelmed, bored, etc. you feel affects what choices you make and how you act.

So you see, all this sensory input and processing really affects what you do all day long. From learning to opportunities to making choices. And to think you didn't even know any of this was happening!

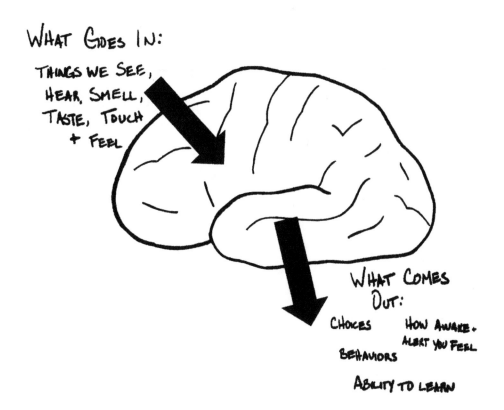

WHAT GOES IN:
THINGS WE SEE, HEAR, SMELL, TASTE, TOUCH + FEEL

WHAT COMES OUT:
CHOICES    HOW AWAKE + ALERT YOU FEEL
BEHAVIORS
ABILITY TO LEARN

# Workbook Section:
# Brain Exec Activity – How You Act and Make Choices

Thinking about your sensory systems and what you like and don't like, what are some things that you like and choose to do, and what are some that you avoid because you don't like them? For instance, maybe you choose to wear a satin shirt because you love the way it feels so soft on your skin or maybe you refuse to wear that wool sweater your grandpa gave you because it is so itchy.

_____

_____

_____

_____

_____

Can you think of a place other than the library or recess where everyone kind of acts the same? Do you act like everyone else there or do you usually act differently? Draw it out in the space here:

# Workbook Section: Brain Dump

Is your brain exploding with all this new knowledge?! Take a minute and write down all the new stuff that you just learned about your brain and sensory systems.

_____

_____

_____

_____

_____

_____

_____

_____

_____

_____

_____

_____

_____

_____

_____

_____

_____

Sensory Modulation

# So, What Exactly is Sensory Modulation?

All right, now that you get what all this sensory stuff is, how you get it, what your brain does with it, and why it's important, it's time you learn about a key player in all this called "Sensory Modulation." Let's get started by breaking down the words again.

*Sensory* – Pretty sure you know what this is by now.

*Modulation* – Modulation means to adjust something so that it is more or less, higher or lower, louder or quieter, etc., to make it more suitable for the situation. One way to think about modulation is turning the volume up or down of something that you are listening to (phone, music, television, etc.) to help you understand what you are hearing. Say you are watching a movie that is so quiet you can't really hear it well. You can see people talking on screen, but you can't tell exactly what they are saying. So you grab the remote and click the volume up (modulate it to be louder, if you will), and with just that little change, all of the sudden the entire experience of watching the movie is better, because, well, you can actually hear what they are saying. Okay, but what if, on the other hand, the volume is so loud that it is blaring out the speakers, hurting your ears, and all you can really do is hold your hands over your ears and look around for the nearest exit? Can you understand what they are saying in the movie? Forget it. Fortunately, you're a mastermind and you grab the remote and quickly click the volume down. Ahhhhhhh, much better. (Thanks, modulation!)

# Workbook Section: Executive Experiment

Your turn to modulate! Grab a smart phone and snap a selfie. Okay, now look at the picture you took on your phone and go to "edit" so we can make some changes. (Remember, modulation = making changes or adjustments.) If you look through all the different changes you can make, like brightness or contrast, you will find one that is labeled "saturation." Choose that one. Now you can *modulate* the saturation to adjust how much color is in your photo. You can decrease the amount of color until you have a black and white photo, or you can increase the amount of color until it is fantastically and vibrantly bright. It's the same photo, but you adjust, or *modulate*, it to make it look different. Now do you get modulation?

# Sensory Modulation and Your Brain

Your brain and body modulate the sensory information coming in from your environment and your body to help it be not too much or not too little.[3,5,6] You may not realize it, but your brain is always trying to adjust the "volume" on stuff that you are seeing, hearing, and feeling. I am telling you: your brain is constantly busy doing stuff you didn't even know about! So the way this works for sensory modulation is that as sensory information travels up to your brain, and even once it gets there, it can be *modulated*, or adjusted toward just right instead of too much or too little.[3,6] This is all super important because our brains work the best when they get just the right amount of info. And Brain Execs are all about helping our brains to work their best.

When I think about sensory modulation, I like to picture a tiny, little security team, kind of like a security team at an airport, a baseball game, or a concert. Except that this security team lives inside your body and brain and decides how much sensory information to let up to the brain. It *modulates* the sensory information, helping your brain get a just-right amount of the just-right stuff.

**BRAIN SECURITY TEAM**

Part of what your brain security team does is work to let in the "right amount" of sensory information for whatever you are doing. Think about a football game in a huge stadium. There is a certain number of seats in the stadium, right? Well, it's the security team's job to make sure that all of the people with tickets get in to fill those seats but not to let too many in.

Your brain security team also works to "turn up" your attention on the important stuff to help you notice and understand it better and "turn down" your attention on the unimportant stuff so that you can ignore it.[5,7] I like to think of this as the security team letting the important sensory stuff get to the attention part of your brain. This is sort of like the security team at a football game letting the people go to the right places. For instance, the players get to go to the field so everyone can pay attention to what they do, but the spectators don't go to the field; they go to the seats instead.

What exactly does modulation in your brain look like? Just like a security team at a concert lets in people with a ticket but blocks out other people, when a brain is working at its best, it blocks out the unimportant stuff and lets the important stuff in.[5,7] It does this because there are so many things happening all around and inside you, all at once, all the time, and if your brain tried to pay attention to it all, it would be on overload. But also, if there was nothing happening, your brain would be bored. It wants it to be just right, and we want it to be just right too because when it is, it can work at its best, which means we can be our best. And this is good because, last time I checked, we are pretty awesome.

When your brain's security team is working at its best and lets in all the important stuff but not a lot of the extras, you feel awake and alert and pay attention to what you are doing without being distracted by a lot of other stuff.[5,7] This might look like you paying attention and learning in class, reading a great book and not being distracted by what is going on around you, playing baseball in the center field position and being locked in on the game, or maybe even crushing it on your favorite video game. (Told you this whole sensory stuff could make you a better gamer, didn't I?)

# Workbook Section: Brain Exec Activity – Modulation and Your Brain Security Team

Are you surprised to hear that your brain has a security team? Draw your Brain Exec Security Team in the space here.

What about when sensory modulation isn't working so well? If you too much sensory info, then there is too much going into your brain, and it can get distracted, overwhelmed, or stressed out by it all.[5,7] Maybe you are trying to pay attention in class, but you can't because you are noticing the trees outside the window, or someone tapping their foot on the other side of the room, or the fact that your shirt is really itchy. Your brain can only pay attention to so many things at once, so if your itchy shirt is super bothering you, you probably can't also pay attention to what your teacher is saying. If this happens, you might miss all the info you are supposed to be learning.

TOO MUCH SENSORY INFO

On the other hand, if your brain security team isn't letting in enough sensory information, then there isn't enough going on in your brain, and it gets bored and might even start getting sleepy or looking for something interesting to

TOO LITTLE SENSORY INFO

wake it up.[3,5,12] Last time I checked, it is super tough to learn something new when you are falling asleep. It's also hard if you are moving around and doing stuff to try to find some interesting sensory info that has nothing to do with what you are supposed to be learning.

So there's a basic overview of sensory modulation and how it can help a brain work at its best. Let's take a closer look at these ideas, because Brain Execs are not "basic overview" people; they are more of the "tell me more, I want to understand exactly how this works" type.

 **Brain Fact:** *Getting the right amount of sensory information to your brain helps it to work at its best.*

# Sensory Modes

To help make sense of Brain Security Team operations, we can classify their work into modes. But first, let's look at exactly what a "mode" is.

A mode is basically a different way of doing something. Think about it this way: when you are going to do something, say, travel from Florida to New York, you could consider the different ways that you could get there, or the different *modes* of travel. For instance, you could go by plane, by car, by bus, or by train. Each of these is a mode of travel to get from Florida to New York.

Here is another example that may be more familiar, but instead of me just telling you about it, you are going to do it!

# Workbook Section: Brainy Experiment

Grab a smart phone and open the camera app again. Now, point the camera at something in the room—a book, a picture, your dog Sam, who is sleeping next to you. Anything will do.

Now, let's look at different ways that the camera on our smart phone can capture that picture, or you could say, the *different modes* we can use to capture that picture. You can start by taking a picture in the regular-ole' photo mode. Got it? Okay, but now what if you swipe left or right? Can you use video mode to take a short video of that same thing? Or what about portrait mode? If you use that mode, you end up with a photo of the exact same object, but it looks a little different, right? Nice job! Does your smart phone have a panoramic mode? You can try that to get another photo that is a little different. You did the same thing in a different way because you used a different *mode*.

Okay, do you get modes now? You can use different modes to do that same thing in a different way. Now, back to the sensory brain stuff …

Brains can work in modes too. It doesn't exactly work like your phone when you can just swipe right and change it, but it is similar in that people's brains can do one thing in different ways.

The way that your Brain Security Team works can determine what sensory mode you are in. In fact, you are about to learn about four sensory modes, and they are each named for how much sensory input your brain security team allows in. They are called "Sensory Just Right," "Sensory Too Much," "Sensory Not Enough," and "Sensory Not Enough, Seeking," and they affect how you experience the sensory stuff that is going on around and inside you.

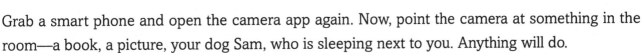

# Workbook Section:
# Brain Exec Activity – Sensory Mode Brainstorm

Think about what you already know about sensory processing and modulation. Can you make any guesses about the four sensory modes before you read further? Write down or draw out any ideas below.

Before we dive in and start learning more about these modes, there is something super important that you need to know: none of the modes is better or worse than any other. They are just different. They all have their strengths and challenges, which we will look at a bit more later. And everyone's just-right is different. What might be just right for me could be too much for you. Or what your bestie thinks is not enough might be your just right. Nobody is wrong here; we are all just different! And learning about what makes you *you* can be really helpful in helping you be the best you.

# Sensory Just Right

Before we examine what happens when our brain security team blocks too much or not enough input, let's not forget that sometimes it works *just right*. When you are in Sensory Just Right mode, your brain gets all the information it needs from the world around you and inside you, but not a bunch of extra. Basically, the info that you are getting matches what you need in the moment.[3,5] This happens because in Just Right mode, your security team lets in a "just right" amount of information, screens the incoming sensory information, and decides what to let in based on whether it is important for whatever  you are doing.[3,5,7,13] If it is important, the team lets it into your brain. If it is not, the team blocks it out. This ability to filter out the unimportant information makes it easier to focus on what *is* important, because only important stuff is getting in.

Let's take a closer look at this ability to filter information in Just Right mode. Say you are in your backyard reading a book. Your security team is letting in all of the words that you see on the pages so that you can read them. Obviously, the words are important information. There are airplanes flying in the sky overhead, but your security team blocks this out because it has nothing to do with the book you are reading. Not important. But then, while you are reading, you start to feel something crawling up your arm. Ahhh! This information is let in because it is potentially important. It could be a bug of the stinging or biting sort, and in that case you would want to get it off of your arm *fast*. Also, it's important because, gross—bugs. Thanks, security team, for letting this info in!

In additon to helping you pay attention to the important stuff, Just Right mode helps you stay in a just-right state of alertness and arousal. Remember the RAS—how when there is sensory information coming through, its job is to tell the brain to wake up and be alert? Well, in Just Right mode, a just-right amount of info moves through, so the RAS tells the brain a just-right amount of times to be awake and alert. This helps you to be awake enough to focus and pay attention, but also to not feel overwhelmed.[3,5]

Another key part of being in Just Right mode is that when opportunities come your way, you notice them.[26] This is because your brain counts opportunities as important information, so the security team lets it in. For example, maybe while you are reading in your yard, you hear the ice cream truck coming down the road. Opportunity to get ice cream?! *Very important!* Ummm, hello, stop reading and go get a treat!

 **Brain Fact:** *When you are in Just Right mode, you are able to notice opportunities around you so that you don't miss out on great things. Like ice cream.*

This leads us into making choices in Just Right mode. When you are able to notice the opportunities around you, you can make a choice to do them. But making decisions in Just Right mode is more than that. Since your brain isn't being overwhelmed by too much sensory information, feeling drowsy because it doesn't have enough, or feeling the need to seek out more, it has the time and energy to make decisions to do things.

If the music is playing and you feel like dancing, you can choose to dance. If all your friends are going to a carnival and you want to go, you can choose to go. If you have a really important question during a test, you can choose to whisper when you ask your teacher. Just Right mode helps all of these things happen.

In Just Right mode, you can match your behaviors to whatever you are doing, which is great because this really helps you to do whatever it is that you are doing and to do it well.[3,16] Think back to that example comparing behavior in the library and at recess. If you are in Just Right mode in the library, you will notice that everyone is being quiet, and you will match that behavior by working quietly also. Just Right mode at recess will let you notice that everyone else is playing an intense game of kickball, focusing on the game, cheering, running, and, of course, kicking. What do you do? Join right in and help your team win!

# Executive Recap: Sensory Just Right

In Sensory Just Right mode, your brain security team:

- Lets in the important information
- Blocks out unimportant information

When you are operating in Just Right mode, you:

- Feel awake and alert
- Can focus and concentrate
- Notice opportunities around you
- Are free to make choices based on what you want to do or should do, because an overwhelmed or underwhelmed brain is not influencing your ability to
- Can engage in behaviors that match what you are doing

# Executive Explanation
# Just Right versus Perfect

We said that when your brain security team is working in Just Right mode, you are getting all the important info but not a lot of the extras. That is totally true, but your security team can make small mistakes while keeping you in Just Right mode. It doesn't have to be perfect. In fact, Just Right mode involves making small adjustments so that you stay "just right." For example, you may be paying attention to what the teacher is saying in class when someone walks by the classroom door. You notice them walking by, but then you turn your attention back to your teacher and keep learning. Just because you noticed something extra for a second doesn't mean your security team isn't on the job. I like to think of this type of scenario as the security team letting something in the door to my brain but then kicking it back out right away when it realizes it is not important.

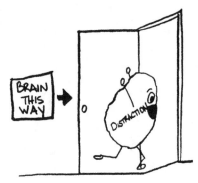

A "Just Right" security team can also accidentally block out important information for a second but then realize the mistake and quickly let it in. This is what happens when you zone out for a sec in class but then jump right back in and keep learning.

# Workbook Section:
# Brain Exec Activity – Just Right Mode

Can you think of a time that you have felt like you were in Just Right mode? Describe what was happening and how you felt. You can write about it or draw it out.

## Sensory Too Much

Now that we know what Sensory Just Right mode looks like, let's talk about what happens in Sensory Too Much mode. Your brain security team does two main things differently in Sensory Too Much mode. For one, it lets in too much sensory information. It's like the door to your brain is left open and the security team keeps inviting everyone in, even though there is already too much going on in there.

Sometimes a security team invites all kinds of information in at once.[7,16] For instance, they might let in the sound of a fan, the feeling of a hard chair, the smell of someone's perfume, and the sight of a flickering light all at the same time. But a lot of times security teams let in too much of a particular kind of information.[3,16] This makes whatever they are letting in too much of seem bigger, louder, brighter, stronger, harder, sharper, itchier, dizzier, or more than it really is.[3,16] If your team lets in too much sound, a sudden noise like a dish dropping or an alarm going off could sound epically loud, which can really startle you and be quite scary! Or perhaps your security team lets in too much vestibular information. If this is the case, when you get on a swing during recess and swing just a little, your brain gets a ton of movement info and you feel like you are on a gargantuan rollercoaster. Excuse me, where is a barf bag?

But that's not the only difference in how your brain security team operates when you are in Too Much mode. Remember how in Just Right mode the security team would filter sensory info and only let in the important stuff? In Too Much mode they don't really check if what they are letting in is important or not, and this can make it very difficult to pay attention to whatever *is* important.[3,5,7]

Say you and your friends are discussing the fact that rats laugh when they are tickled. While your besties are talking, your brain security team lets in their voices but also keeps letting in other stuff. Like maybe the feeling of the tag in the back of your shirt or the super bright sun in your face that is hurting your eyes. You are trying to pay attention to what they are saying, but your brain is letting in so much of the "other stuff" that it is keeping you from focusing on the important thing: your friend telling you about these rats.

(BTW, it is totally true about rats laughing when they are tickled. I highly recommend watching a video of this because it is hilarious. I do not, however, recommend actually catching a rat and trying to tickle it, because gross.)

In addition to making it difficult to pay attention and focus on the right things, at times all of this extra sensory input to your brain in Too Much mode may make you feel overwhelmed, feel like you need to get away for a bit, and maybe even feel agitated. Sometimes getting too much sensory info has an even stronger effect. When this happens, it can make your body go into a state that we call "Fight or Flight."[3,7,16] This is basically your brain thinking there is a real threat, panicking, and getting ready to either fight the threat off or run away from it. We will learn more about this later, along with how to help your brain out when it happens, but for now it is enough to know that if you ever get too much sensory information at once and you feel aggressive or like you need to get away from the situation really fast, it is likely because you are in Too Much mode and your brain thinks that it needs to fight off something or run away from it.

As we see in all modes, Sensory Too Much mode affects your alertness and arousal.[3,10] In this mode, your RAS does the same job (telling your brain to be awake and alert when sensory info moves through)[9] but your security team lets in too much sensory info. As a result, your RAS has to keep telling the brain to wake up and be alert over and over again because sensory info keeps moving through. Sometimes it even yells really loud to your brain. *WAKE UP, BRAIN!* But the thing is, your brain is *already* awake and alert! As a result, your brain gets SUPER alert and aroused. This can make you feel jittery, on-edge, fidgety, worried, anxious, fearful, and like you are waiting for something to happen (like a really loud noise, perhaps). Depending on how your brain security team is operating and how your brain responds, you could feel these things in a little way or in a really big way.

And of course, this all affects the opportunities that you notice around you, the choices that you make, and the behaviors that you engage in.[3,11,26] Maybe your friends are all talking during lunch and planning to get together this weekend, but the noises and smells in the lunchroom are overwhelming and you can't pay attention to the conversation. You totally miss out on the opportunity for a fun weekend because you were so distracted and overwhelmed, you didn't even hear about it. Or maybe your uncle went to Hawaii and brought you back this awesome surf shirt that is really cool, but you keep choosing to not wear it because it is super-bright neon orange and it hurts your eyes all day when you have it on. Or maybe your friends are going to an amusement park and invite you, but you super do not like the feeling of rollercoasters and rides, even little ones, so you choose not to go.

Behaviors during Sensory Too Much mode are often just an output of how you feel, and you might be feeling distracted, overwhelmed, agitated, mad, or scared. This can make you act grumpy, cranky, or nervous, and if you are in Fight or Flight mode you might even push or yell. It's not that you mean to; it just seems to happen.

If you are reading any of this and thinking, "That is totally me!" then good news: being a Brain Executive doesn't only mean *understanding* the brain; it means that you learn to *manage* it so that it works a bit better. So keep reading because there is help on the way!

## Executive Recap: Sensory Too Much

In Sensory Too Much mode, your brain security team:
- Lets in too much sensory information
- Does not filter out unimportant information

When you are operating in Too Much mode, you might:
- Feel over-alert
- Have a hard time focusing and concentrating because you are distracted by other sensory input
- Miss important information and opportunities because you are distracted by other sensory input
- Hear, see, feel, taste, or smell things more than others
- Feel overwhelmed by sensory input
- Feel agitated, cranky, or scared because of sensory input

# Workbook Section:
# Brain Exec Activity – Too Much Mode

Can you think of a time that you have felt like you were in Sensory Too Much mode? Describe what was happening and how you felt. You can write about it or draw it out.

PS: It's okay if you can't think of a time that you were in Too Much mode. Your brain security team may be better at blocking information than letting it in.

# Sensory Not Enough

If Sensory Too Much happens when your security team lets too much sensory information into your brain, Sensory Not Enough is exactly the opposite. It occurs when your security team *blocks out* too much info so that *not enough* gets to your brain. In this mode, there is sensory information waiting to get into your brain, but your security team won't let it in.

What does this mean for paying attention to important stuff going on around you and inside you? Well, the brain is where attention happens, so to pay attention to something, it has to get up to your brain.

Solve the riddle to answer the question:

**IF** attention happens in the brain …

**AND** in Sensory Not Enough mode, your brain security team blocks sensory info from getting to your brain …

**THEN** when you are operating in Sensory Not Enough mode, are you able to pay attention to the info in the world around you and inside you?

If you answered "no," Executive Detective, you are right! When you are in Not Enough mode, it is really hard to pay attention to things going on around and inside you[3,13,16] because the sensory information that is supposed to tell you about that stuff isn't getting into your brain. The sounds around you might not be getting up to your brain. The things around you that you can see might not be getting up there either. Or smells or tastes. Or feelings of things that touch your skin. Or even information from your vestibular and proprioceptive systems about how your body is moving. All of this stuff is real and happening, but you can't really pay attention to it because it never gets up to your brain.

Similar to Sensory Too Much mode, your security team can block out too much of different kinds of sensory information at once, but it can also block out too much of just one kind. For instance, you might be able to pay attention to things you are seeing around you, but your security team is blocking out things that you are hearing, like your teacher's voice. You know she is talking, but her voice isn't coming through that well. Since you aren't getting much info from her talking, you stop paying attention to what she is saying. Maybe you start feeling bored and sleepy, or maybe you start looking at cool stuff around your because your brain is getting information from your eyes just fine.

**Brain Fact:** *Your security team can block out different kinds of sensory information at once, but it can also block out just one kind. This means you might be getting plenty of one kind of sensory information but not enough of a different kind.*

Don't miss an important fact from this scenario: You are supposed to be learning what that teacher is saying, but her voice isn't coming through very clearly because your security team is blocking it out. How easy is it going to be to learn in this situation? You might be a super-smart kid, but you also might flunk the test because you weren't able to really listen to what the teacher was saying. This is why it is so important to be a Brain Executive and learn about your sensory patterns and how to help your brain!

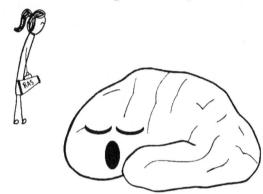

How does it feel to be in Not Enough mode? For one, it is hard to pay attention to what is going on. Also, without enough sensory information coming in, you can feel bored, lethargic, and sleepy.[3,16] What exactly does "lethargic" mean? It means that you are sluggish or moving slow, that you don't have a lot of energy, and that you are feeling tired and perhaps sleepy. Remember our friend the RAS and how every time your security team lets in sensory information, your RAS shouts up to your brain to be awake and alert?[3,9] Well, in Not Enough mode, your team doesn't let in much sensory info, so your RAS doesn't end up telling your brain to be awake and alert very often. Since your brain isn't being told to stay awake and alert, it doesn't. Instead, it might feel sleepy and lethargic.

 **Brain Fact:** *If your RAS is not telling your brain to be awake and alert, it goes into default resting mode. This makes you feel lethargic and sleepy.*

What does all of this mean for noticing opportunities? If you are in Not Enough mode, are you going to get the sensory information that tells you about opportunities around you? No, probably not.[16] If your security team blocks out the feeling of your friend tapping you on the shoulder, you might miss your turn in a wild game of kickball. If your security team blocks out the sound of your brother yelling "Pizza is here!" you might miss out on a delicious dinner. If your security team blocks out the feeling of moving around really fast, you might miss out on exactly how much fun it is to spin on a tire swing.

The choices that you make are affected too. In Sensory Not Enough mode, when given a choice between options, you might notice that you often choose whatever gives more sensory input. For instance, you might choose spicy jalapeno or intense ranch chips rather than plain old salt ones. Or you might want the neon green binder instead of the regular green one. On the other hand, you might notice that in Sensory Not Enough mode you don't really care that much about choices. Sometimes this is because you aren't feeling very awake and alert or you aren't noticing things well, so you are having trouble paying attention to what the choices really are.

And last but not least, let's talk about behaviors that are commonly linked with Not Enough mode. It's important to remember that in this mode your RAS is not telling your brain to wake up, so you are feeling overall bored, lethargic, and sleepy. And you are missing out on important information. How does someone like this usually act? They might be slumped down in their chair, looking like they aren't paying attention; they probably aren't talking or moving a lot; they may not respond when someone says their name or asks them a question; and sometimes they look like they are "zoned out" or don't care.[3,5,16] It's not that they *actually* don't care; they are just having trouble staying alert and attentive.

If you think this describes you, keep reading, because there are lots of ways to help your brain wake up!

## Executive Recap: Not Enough

In the Sensory Not Enough mode, your brain security team:
- Does not let in enough sensory information
- Lets in unimportant information

When you are operating in Not Enough mode, you might:
- Feel bored
- Feel lethargic, tired, or sleepy
- Have a hard time focusing and concentrating
- Miss important information and opportunities because they don't make it up to your brain
- Hear, see, feel, taste, or smell things less than others
- Move or talk slowly or not a lot
- Look to others like you don't care about what is going on

# Workbook Section:
# Brain Exec Activity – Not Enough Mode

Can you think of a time that you have felt like you were in Sensory Not Enough mode? Describe what was happening and how you felt. You can write about it or draw it out!

PS: It's okay if you can't think of a time that you were in Not Enough mode. Your brain security team may be better at letting information in than blocking it out.

# Sensory Not Enough, Seeking

You may have noticed that there is only a one-word difference between Sensory Not Enough mode and Sensory Not Enough, Seeking mode. You may even be thinking that since the names are similar, the modes might have some similarities too. If you are thinking this, you are right! Hey, you're getting pretty good at this brain stuff …

NOT ENOUGH

The brain security team actually acts the same in both modes—they block out too much sensory information so that the brain doesn't get enough. The difference between the modes is how your brain responds to not having enough sensory information.[3,5,11] In Not Enough mode, your brain just accepts that there is not enough sensory info coming in. It chills out, maybe zones out, and goes with feeling lethargic. In Not Enough, Seeking mode your brain says, "Hey! There is not enough sensory info coming in and I need it. I better get busy and try to find some!" So your brain makes your body go into overdrive to try to find sensory input. It *seeks* it out.

NOT ENOUGH SEEKING →

 **Brainy Word Alert:** *What exactly does "seeking" mean? To seek means to try to find something, to hunt for something, or to search for something. It is a very active word. You are definitely not just sitting there chilling out in Seeking mode. You are on the go, trying to find whatever it is you are looking for. And of course, in Sensory Seeking mode, you are seeking sensory input for your brain.*

Here's the thing: your brain knows that when you are alive and awake, certain things are supposed to be happening. You are supposed to be seeing, hearing, tasting, smelling, and feeling. Your brain is literally programed to know that these things should happen.[13] So if you are alive and awake (which I hope that you are right now), and your security team is blocking out too much sensory info, your brain might say, "Wait a minute! This isn't right! We should be getting sensory info, and if we are not, I am going to find some!" That's Seeking mode.

I like to think about the brain in Sensory Not Enough, Seeking mode (AKA Seeking mode) as being "hungry," except instead of being hungry for food, it is hungry for sensory input. Have you ever been hanging out at home and started to feel hungry? What did you do? You probably went into the kitchen and started looking for something to eat. This is basically what your brain does in Seeking mode, but of course it is looking for sensory input, not food.

So how do you find and get more sensory input? That depends on what type of sensory information you are looking for. If it is sound that you need, you might turn on some music and turn the volume up loud. If it is visual information that you need, you might watch something that is moving, like a fan or cars going by, or maybe you look around until you find something with bright colors or fantastically wild patterns to look at. If it is taste or smell that you are looking for, you might eat something spicy, salty, or sour, and while you are eating it you breathe deeply to take in all the smell. For touch, you might run your hands and fingers over different surfaces like a rug or a marble or maybe even some sandpaper. Because vestibular information tells you about your body moving, if you are seeking vestibular input you might run, jump, spin, or do any other action that moves your head around. And last but not least, for proprioceptive input you might do things that make your muscles and joints work hard, like squeezing your pencil really tightly while you write or pushing down hard as you form the letters. (Anyone ever broken a pencil doing this???)

Notice that for all of these examples, you are *actively* doing something to get more sensory input. There is no just sitting and chilling. People who are operating in Seeking mode are usually *very* active and busy. These are the people who cannot sit still, are always on the go, are touching everything, playing loud music, and in general doing *a lot*.

Let's talk about some of the brain-science specifics for this mode, because Seeking mode is a little tricky. For one, if your security team is blocking sensory information, then your RAS is not shouting up to the brain to be awake and alert, right? So you would think that you would feel sleepy and lethargic like we see in Not Enough mode. But that is not the case at all. In Seeking mode, your brain sort of overrides this sleepy/lethargic state and instead gets the body active so that it can seek more sensory input. You are definitely not focused and attentive like in Just Right mode, but you aren't chilling like in Not Enough mode either. Seeking mode is characterized by a lot of movement and activity but not a lot of focused attention. This mode can be pretty chaotic.

Also, you might think that in this mode you would notice all of the information around you because you are looking for it, but don't forget that your security team is *blocking out* sensory input. You actually end up missing a lot of information in Seeking mode for two reasons: 1. because your security team is blocking it out, and 2. because you are so busy looking for certain sensory input that you don't notice other stuff.

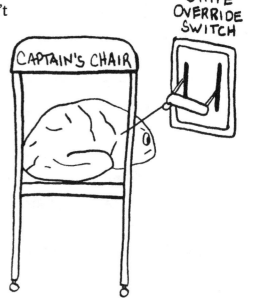

How are opportunities, choices, and behaviors affected? Once again, we see that opportunities are missed. (Side note: have you noticed that you miss opportunities in every mode except for Just Right mode?) In Seeking mode, you miss out on opportunities because you don't notice them, and perhaps you are distracted by trying to find the right sensory input for your brain.

The choices you make reflect the fact that you are mostly just trying to seek out sensory info. If given a choice between doing something with only a little sensory input (reading, for instance) or doing something with a lot of sensory input (perhaps playing a game of basketball in the gym with the music blaring), you are definitely going to pick the one with lots of sensory input.

As for behavior, well, behavior can be pretty chaotic and active in Seeking mode. In fact, people in this mode often end up getting in trouble for moving too much, fidgeting too much, or being distracted. People in Seeking mode can even be seen as daredevils or risk-takers because they like to do things that are pretty intense to get sensory input.[16] Examples of this can be crashing into walls or furniture on purpose, jumping off high surfaces, swinging incredibly high on the playground, or riding their bike super fast.

# Executive Recap: Not Enough, Seeking

In the Sensory Not Enough, Seeking mode, your brain security team:

- Does not let in enough sensory information AND your brain gets active to seek out sensory input

When you are operating in Seeking mode, you might:

- Move around a lot to get vestibular and proprioceptive information
- Turn on something that makes noise and turn the volume up loud
- Touch a lot of different items, fabrics, and surfaces
- Get captivated looking at something that is moving fast or is very bright
- Taste and smell strong flavors and scents
- Have a hard time focusing and concentrating because you are busy seeking out sensory input
- Miss important information and opportunities because they don't make it up to your brain and because you are busy seeking

If any of this sounds familiar and you are thinking you might be a Sensory Seeker, keep reading! There are lots of ways to help your brain get more of the sensory input that it needs.

# Workbook Section:
# Brain Exec Activity – Not Enough, Seeking Mode

Can you think of a time that you have felt like you were in Sensory Not Enough, Seeking mode? Describe what was happening and how you felt. You can write about it or draw it out!

PS: It's okay if you can't think of a time that you were in Seeking mode. Your brain might not be the type that gets active to try to find sensory info.

# Workbook Section:
# Brain Dump

Is your brain exploding with all this new knowledge?! Take a minute and write down all the new stuff that you just learned about your brain and sensory systems.

# Workbook Section:
# Brain Exec Activity – Strengths and Challenges

Like we said before, none of the sensory modes is better or worse than any other. They are just different, and they all have their strengths and challenges. Let's take a closer look at what those strengths and challenges are. Below are some basic thoughts for each pattern. Can you list at least one more strength and challenge for each?

| | Strength | Challenge |
|---|---|---|
| **Just Right** | Can often act as expected because your sensory input is about what is expected | At times may not notice as much, be as chill, or try to seek out some fun input as others do |
| **Too Much** | Notices opportunities and cool stuff that others don't | At times may become overwhelmed |
| **Not Enough** | Can be super chill in environments that are chaotic | May have difficulty staying alert and focused |
| **Not Enough, Seeking** | Is often the person who wants to try everything and finds ways to have fun | May have a hard time during activities where you are supposed to be still and quiet |

Sensory
Patterns

# Sensory Patterns

You know what patterns are, right? Things that happen in a certain way over and over again. Lots of things in life occur in patterns, and because they occur in the same way each time, they help us to know what will probably happen next. Take the seasons, for example. Because seasons happen in the same order every year and each season has specific weather, we can make predictions, or educated guesses, about what type of weather will happen next. For instance, in the Northern Hemisphere, winter is cold and is followed by spring, which will bring warmer temperatures. After the spring, it will be summer, and the weather will become hot.

Patterns can also help us to predict how we will act at certain times. Daily schedules in the classroom occur in patterns and influence how we act in class. Maybe your school day starts with reading, a time during which everyone is pretty quiet. In the middle of the day is lunch-time, which is totally loud and busy, and after that is math so everyone has to quiet back down and focus. Because of the patterns, you can predict that most people are going to talk more during lunch than during math.

Your Brain Security Team works in patterns, or predictable ways, too, so there is a pattern to your sensory modes. To figure out your sensory patterns, we have to look at each of your senses (sight, hearing, vestibular, etc.) and think of how your Brain Security Team usually operates for them. For instance, your Brain Security Team may typically let in too much sound, so you are usually a Too Much mode for sound. If it does, you have a pattern of being over-responsive to sounds. This means that you can predict things like: when you go see a movie in a theatre, the sound will be too loud for you, or if you are in a really noisy environment with lots of different and loud sounds, you will likely feel aggitated, nervous, or overwhelmed.

On the other hand, if your Brain Security Team usually blocks out too much sound, you have a sensory pattern of being a Not Enough or Seeker for sound. You can predict things like when all of your friends are listening to the newest best-song-ever, you will want to turn it up even louder or if the adult-in-charge is giving directions to a group, you might not hear them. It's a pattern of needing more sound.

 **Brain Fact:** *Your Brain Security Team works in patterns, or predictable ways, so there is a pattern to your sensory modes.*

## ✿ Brain Exec Activity – Patterns and Predictions ✿

Patterns are things that happen over and over again in the same way, which means that we can use them to make predictions about what will happen next. Make predictions to complete the patterns below.

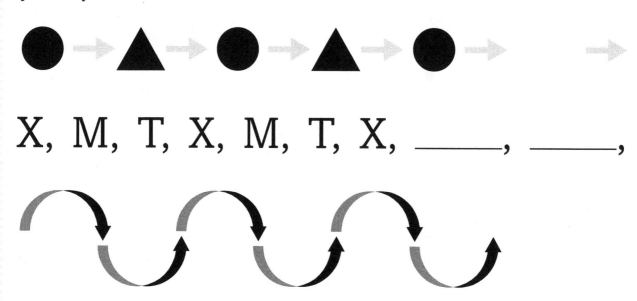

X, M, T, X, M, T, X, \_\_\_\_, \_\_\_\_,

Sensory patterns can help us to know and predict how we will respond to sensory input. Like maybe you always startle at loud noises such as the bell at school. Or maybe you always fall asleep if you sit too long during class.

# Finding Your Own Sensory Patterns

While you read, you may have started to figure out what your own sensory patterns are. Now it is time to take a closer look. The next pages have a lot of statements about how you might experience sensory information. Read each statement and highlight the ones that describe you. Pay attention to words like "often," "not usually," "a lot," or "more than others." You may find a statement that describes something you've done maybe once or twice, but if it says "often," then only highlight it if you have done what it says *often*. For instance, maybe it says, "I often gag when I try new foods." If you can think of a bunch of times that you have gagged trying new foods, then highlight that sentence. But if you can only think of that one time that you gagged on Aunt Ellie's dried-out fruit cake, well, one time is not *often*, so don't highlight it. Make sense? Also, highlight the shapes next to the statement that describe you. At the end of each section, you will add up the number of highlighted shapes that you have.

And one more really important thing: you need to answer these questions with the help of your Chief Advisor, the trusted adult you are reading this book with. This is someone who knows you well and can help you see how you respond to sensory situations, even if sometimes you aren't aware of it. They are also a person who can help make sure you are paying attention to the words like "often."

 ## A Note for the Adult Chief Advisor

You have an important role in the completion of the questionnaire! Your job is to guide the Exec as they read these statements, helping them to understand and consider what is presented in the words. This may mean asking leading questions or having a discussion about sensory characteristics. It may also be helpful to help the reader think of specific examples of how they have responded to sensory input in real life. In addition, you might need to help the reader pay attention to the frequency of words and phrases like "often," "not usually," or "a lot." As you support the Executive through this process, remember that your role is to be a guide and a listener, not a "teller." Allow the child to be the expert on themselves and make sure that you are honoring this process as they give voice to how they feel and experience sensation. As the adult, it can be easy to tell the child how they are feeling, but your perception of how they feel, based on your own perspectives and sensory patterns, may not be accurate.

Please remember that this questionnaire is not intended or designed to be a clinical assessment of sensory patterns, as that can only take place with the direct support of a professional clinician. That being said, this questionnaire was designed specifically to provide insight into the reader's sensory patterns and to help inform yourself and the reader about sensory characteristics. See the section near the end of the book about finding direct professional support if you feel that you and your child need additional help in discovering, understanding, or managing sensory patterns.

 ## A Note for Clinicians

If you are a clinician guiding the reader through this book, you have likely already completed a sensory-based assessment and have standardized results. Don't skip this portion! The goal of completing the questionnaire is for the reader to develop an understanding of their sensory patterns and characteristics. Considering each statement and deciding if it applies to them is a key exercise in building this self-awareness.

# Sensory Pattern Questionnaire – Vision

Highlight the sentence, along with the shape, that **best** describes you.

| | |
|---|---|
| If my room is really messy with items out of place and scattered everywhere (for example, clothing on the floor or a lot of stuff spread out on a table), I feel bothered and sometimes overwhelmed. | ▲ |
| I don't really notice whether my room is messy or neat. | ■ |
| I prefer my room to be messy with items scattered around and misplaced in unexpected spots. I like the way that it looks all busy and messy. | ★ |
| I seem like most kids when it comes to how neat or messy my room is. It gets messy sometimes and sometimes it stays neat … I do notice this, but either way doesn't really bother me. | ● |
| *A note here, Exec … having a messy room because you don't feel like cleaning it is different than your room being messy because of your sensory patterns. When choosing the sentence that best fits you, think about if you notice when your room is messy, if it bothers you or makes you feel overwhelmed, or if you actually really like the way it looks and feels when it is messy.* | |

Highlight the sentence, along with the shape, that **best** describes you.

| | |
|---|---|
| I really like when things in a familiar room change and look new. I am always wanting to redecorate, move things, add new things, or somehow change up how a room looks. | ★ |
| If I walk into a familiar room and there is a new decoration or item in it, I often don't notice right away. In fact, sometimes I don't notice until someone points it out. | ■ |
| I am usually the first to notice a new item or decoration in a familiar room, even if it is a small change. I prefer for things to just stay the same. | ▲ |
| I notice new things in familiar rooms, like a new decoration. It doesn't bother me, and in fact I even like it sometimes. I seem to react about the same as most others do to new things. | ● |

# HOW TO BE A BRAIN EXECUTIVE

Highlight **each** sentence, along with the shape, that describes you.

Bright lights really bother me. I often cover my eyes or squint. ▲

When other people say that the light is too bright, like outside on a sunny day, I often don't seem to notice the brightness. ■

I really like looking at things with bright lights, colors, and moving parts and will look at them for a long time. ★

I often notice visual things that others don't, like a light flickering. ▲

A lot of times I don't notice things that other people see. ■

Sure, I like to look at things that move like spinning toys, but I don't seem to become so captivated with it that I cannot stop. I seem to want to watch this type of toy about as much as other kids. ●

When I look at a page with a lot of stuff on it, like a maze or a search-and-find, I feel overwhelmed. ▲

When I look at a page with a lot of stuff on it, like a maze or a search-and-find, I tend to be able to focus on what I am looking at and ignore the unimportant things. ●

I often move things just so I can watch them, like jiggling a pencil in my fingers or spinning a coin. ★

I bump into things in my environment, like chairs or a wall, more than others do. I don't seem to notice that they are there. ■

I am usually able to ignore the extra stuff in my environment so that I can focus on and complete the job I am doing. ●

I often bring things really close to my face and look at them there, or I like to look at things from the corner of my vision. ★

Number of ●

Number of ▲

Number of ■

Number of ★

# Sensory Pattern Questionnaire – Hearing

Highlight the sentence, along with the shape, that **best** describes you.

When working in a group where multiple people are talking at once, I also often miss information. It is hard to know whom to pay attention to. If someone tries to get my attention, they may have to say my name more than once. ■

Working in a group where multiple people are talking at once can make me feel overwhelmed and sometimes anxious. All of the voices at once are overwhelming. I do not like it. ▲

I am able to participate in groups where multiple people are talking at once. I can follow the conversation and join in. Even if I get a little frustrated or confused by the noise sometimes, I am generally okay and can keep working with the group. ●

When working in groups, I like it when everyone is talking at once. The sounds can be confusing and I don't always follow the conversation, but I like all of the noise. In fact, the louder and more "all at once" it is, the more I like it. ★

Highlight **each** sentence, along with the shape, that describes you.

When others think the volume is just right, I think it is too loud. ▲

I notice loud sounds, like plates clanking and people talking in the lunchroom, but they don't usually bother me or make me feel nervous. ●

People tell me to "listen" or "pay attention" a lot. ■

Background noises really bother me. They are distracting and sometimes make me feel agitated. ▲

When I am in loud places, like the lunchroom, an amusement park, or a busy store, I am able to notice and respond to important sounds like someone calling my name. ●

I cover my ears to block out sounds at times when others don't. ▲

I often turn the volume up; I just like it that way. ★

I often don't notice things that others hear. ■

People often have to repeat directions to me. ■

In general, I notice when someone says directions to me and don't need them to be repeated more than others do. ●

I like having background noise on and multiple sounds playing at once, like music playing while the TV is on. ★

Loud places like the lunchroom or a busy store bother me and can make me feel overwhelmed or agitated. ▲

I like to put things right next to my ear to hear them louder. I do this more than others do. ★

I make my own noises to listen to by doing something like humming or tapping. I do this more than others do. ★

Unexpected sounds can really scare me and cause me to feel anxiety and fear. ▲

I can zone out even when there are a lot of noises around me. In fact, I do this a lot. ■

I can usually pay attention to the important stuff I should be listening to, even when there are extra sounds around me. ●

| Number of ● | Number of ▲ | Number of ■ | Number of ★ |
| --- | --- | --- | --- |
| | | | |

# Sensory Pattern Questionnaire – Taste

Highlight the sentence, along with the shape, that **best** describes you.

| | |
|---|---|
| Like most kids, I can be sort of picky about trying new foods, but I am usually able to try a little, and when I do, I can tell if I like them or not. | ● |
| I almost always refuse to try new foods, and if I do try, I often gag. | ▲ |
| I like to try new foods. I enjoy how the taste is new and surprising. | ★ |
| I will usually try new foods. When I do, I don't always have an opinion whether I really like them or not. | ■ |

Highlight **each** sentence, along with the shape, that describes you.

| | |
|---|---|
| People say that I am a very picky eater. Sometimes I only like certain brands of foods or will only eat a food if a specific person makes it. | ▲ |
| I don't have very specific food preferences. In general, I will eat most things. I am just not that picky about food. | ■ |
| My food preferences seem like most other kids'. I may be picky sometimes, but I have a variety of foods that are my favorites. | ● |
| I have a set of foods that are my favorites, but in general I can eat other things, even if I don't really like them. | ● |
| I often add extra flavor to my food, like adding salt or spices. | ★ |
| When I have to buy food somewhere, like from the cafeteria, I often cannot find anything that I will eat. Sometimes I just skip that meal. | ▲ |
| A lot of times, I don't really notice flavors that much. | ■ |
| When picking out food, I usually get a plain or bland flavor, like the ones labeled "original," "plain," or "unseasoned." | ▲ |

I am able to notice differences in tastes of food, but I don't panic when there is something different. For instance, if my someone buys a different brand of peanut butter, I notice it and will probably say something, but I will eat it. ●

If you give me two different foods that are similar, I often cannot tell the difference unless I look. ■

When food is too salty or spicy, I often don't notice it, even though other people do. ■

I like to specifically eat the parts of food with the most flavor, like licking off the seasoning of a chip or eating the spicy sausage on pizza. ★

If I am making food or cooking, I can often taste it and decide if it needs more of a certain ingredient. ●

I often taste things that aren't food. I just like to see what stuff tastes like! ★

I have a "set menu" of foods that I like. I prefer to eat only these every day. ▲

When picking out food, I usually get intense flavors like extra bold ranch chips or super sour candy. ★

| Number of ● | Number of ▲ | Number of ■ | Number of ★ |
| --- | --- | --- | --- |
| | | | |

# Sensory Pattern Questionnaire – Smell

Highlight **each** sentence, along with the shape, that describes you.

I don't seem to notice smells as much as other people do.　■

I am usually the first person to notice a smell.　▲

I seem to notice smells about the same as most other people do, not really any more or less.　●

I often notice smells that others don't.　▲

I love to smell different things, in fact, I smell things all the time just to see what they smell like.　★

I often don't know what something is just by smelling it. Like, what is that stinky smell? The trash or the dog? I can't tell the difference between smells very well.　■

You know how sometimes it seems like everyone all of a sudden smells a new smell at the same time? Like when the food starts burning or if someone lights a scented candle? In general, I am part of that group that smells it at the same time.　●

I really like stuff that other people think smells too strongly, like if someone wears too much perfume.　★

Often, someone has to point out a smell to me before I notice.　■

In general, I notice smells, but then I get used to them and don't notice them much anymore. Like if I walk into my grandma's house and it smells like old people…I wrinkle up my nose for the first 10 minutes, but then I mostly forget about it.　●

Other people notice that I smell different things a lot. Sometimes things that you aren't necessarily supposed to smell.　★

Smells often make me gag and feel like I am going to throw up.　▲

Sometimes I can't concentrate because of a smell that is bothering me, even though everyone else seems fine.　▲

When I smell things, I usually put them right up close to my nose so that the smell is the strongest. ★

Smells seems to bother me about the same amount as they bother others, not really any more or any less. ●

Smells that others think are really bad don't really bother me. It might make others gag, but I'm pretty okay with it. ■

I avoid places that have strong smells, like a store with perfumes or the lunchroom. ▲

I often make choices to be closer to smells. For instance, in a store I might stay in the spice or candle aisle or if someone is wearing perfume or cologne, I might move closer. ★

People often say things to me like, "Can't you smell that?!" ■

I am able to use smell to tell me about what is going on around me, like, "Smells like we are having spaghetti tonight," or "Ummm, I think baby bro needs a diaper change." ●

| Number of ● | Number of ▲ | Number of ■ | Number of ★ |
|---|---|---|---|
| | | | |

# Sensory Pattern Questionnaire – Touch

Highlight the sentence, along with the shape, that **best** describes you.

| | |
|---|---|
| If I accidentally get something messy on me, like applesauce or glue, I clean it off immediately. I really, really don't like the feeling of it. | ▲ |
| If I accidentally get something messy on me, like applesauce or glue, I often don't notice it. If I do, it doesn't bother me. In fact, I might forget about it for a while. | ■ |
| If I accidentally get something messy on me, like applesauce or glue, I notice it. I may clean it off right away, or I may let it stay for a while, depending on what I am doing. Either way, it doesn't usually bother me that much or freak me out. | ● |
| If I accidentally get something messy on me, like applesauce or glue, I really like the feel of it. To be honest, I often get more on me on purpose. | ★ |

Highlight the sentence, along with the shape, that **best** describes you.

| | |
|---|---|
| I often don't notice if someone brushes up against me or taps me on the shoulder to get my attention. | ■ |
| I am okay with someone tapping me on the shoulder or arm to get my attention. I notice and respond to it, but it doesn't freak me out. | ● |
| I often startle when someone taps me on the shoulder or arm to get my attention. I wish people wouldn't do this. | ▲ |
| I kind of like it when someone taps me to get my attention, especially if it surprises me and makes me jump. | ★ |

Highlight *each* sentence, along with the shape, that describes you.

| | |
|---|---|
| I often bump into things or brush up against items on purpose because I like how it feels. | ★ |
| I like touching different textures, and I definitely touch things at times to see what they feel like (for instance, touching the fabrics of clothing when I am shopping). I don't seem to touch things more than other people do, though. | ● |
| I often avoid touching things that other people seem okay with. For instance, someone else might want to feel the velvet fabric on a shirt, but I refuse to touch velvet. | ▲ |
| My clothing must be just right, not twisted or too tight anywhere. | ▲ |
| I don't notice if my clothes are twisted on my body. Someone usually has to tell me, or I may notice if I look in a mirror. | ■ |
| I seem to be about the same as other kids my age when it comes to noticing if my clothing is twisted or not lined up correctly. Sure, I miss it sometimes, but I am generally okay at noticing it. | ● |
| I often touch items with only the very tips of my fingers or with the backs of my hands instead of my palm. | ▲ |
| When other people touch something new with just their fingers, I like to dive in with my whole hand. For instance, in science we made slime and at first everyone wanted to feel it carefully, but not me; I picked the whole ball of slime up and squished it through my fingers. | ★ |
| I am often the first person who is willing to touch something new. | ★ |
| My peers can do things like reach into their backpack and feel around to find a pencil without looking. I try but I don't seem to notice the feeling of the different items. Eventually I just have to look to find it. | ■ |
| I avoid walking on different surfaces like grass or sand. I don't like how it feels. | ▲ |
| If I walk from one surface to another, like from the grass to the sand, I often don't even notice. | ■ |
| I love feeling different textures with my feet and will rub my feet or wiggle my toes on things like grass, a blanket, or a bumpy sidewalk just to feel it. I do this often. | ★ |

# Sensory Patterns

I refuse to wear clothing with tags inside or seams that rub. They bother me a lot. ▲

A tag or seam on clothing may bother me, but I can usually continue to wear the clothing. ●

I often don't notice when I get food on my hands and face when eating. People may have to tell me to wipe it off. ■

If I get food on my hands and face while I eat, I am able to notice it most of the time and clean it off. ●

I often fidget with stuff just to feel it, like the bottom of my shirt, pencils in my desk, or the zipper on my backpack. I can fidget with these things over and over again for a long time. I seem to do this more than others do. ★

I enjoy using fidget toys, but I don't have to have them all the time, and after a while I get bored with them. I seem to like them about as much as other kids my age do. ●

I often don't notice if I accidentally bump into something or brush up against an item. ■

Number of ●

Number of ▲

Number of ■

Number of ★

# Sensory Pattern Questionnaire – Vestibular

Highlight **each** sentence, along with the shape, that describes you.

I seem to have a good sense of where I am as I move around a room. I don't run into items like tables or a wall that often. ●

I accidentally bump into items in my environment, like a table or wall, more than other kids do. I can see these things; I just seem to bump into them anyway. ■

I am very scared of heights. Even small heights like the first rung of a ladder makes me nervous. ▲

People describe me as "always on the go." I just seem to want to move around all the time and I have a really hard time sitting still. If I have to stay in place, I fidget and wiggle. ★

I avoid doing activities that require my feet to be off the ground, like swinging, sitting on a high stool, or biking. ▲

I love doing activities when my feet are not touching the ground. I like how it makes me feel sort of unstable. In fact sometimes I do this on purpose, like if I am on a stool, I will put my feet on the rungs and wiggle the stool around. ★

I can keep my balance while standing, even with my eyes closed. ●

I have a very hard time keeping my balance if I close my eyes. ■

I love doing things like walking around or swinging with my eyes closed. I love how it makes you feel sort of weird and off balance. I often close my eyes just so that I can feel this way. ★

I seem to lose my balance more easily that my peers. This can mean that I fall more often. ■

I seem to be able to keep my balance about as is expected for kids my age. Sure, sometimes I get off-balance or fall, but I am usually okay and can even correct my balance before I fall at times. ●

When doing things that involve spinning, I do not seem to get as dizzy as others. ■

I love to do things like spinning, swinging, and riding rollercoasters! I seem to like to do these things more than others do. ★

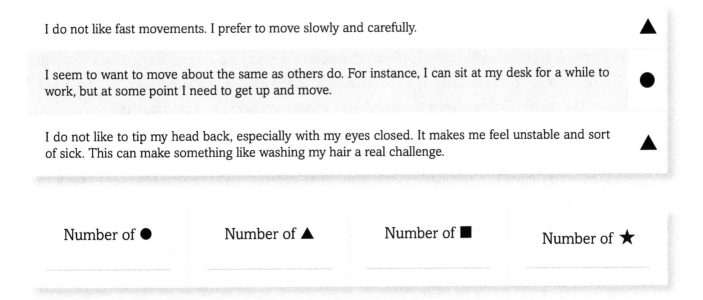

I do not like fast movements. I prefer to move slowly and carefully. ▲

I seem to want to move about the same as others do. For instance, I can sit at my desk for a while to work, but at some point I need to get up and move. ●

I do not like to tip my head back, especially with my eyes closed. It makes me feel unstable and sort of sick. This can make something like washing my hair a real challenge. ▲

Number of ● _____

Number of ▲ _____

Number of ■ _____

Number of ★ _____

# Getting Your Questionnaire Results

Wow! That was a lot of questions to answer! Ready to tally up your shapes and figure out what your sensory patterns are? Drum roll, please …

To do this, look at the number of shapes that you highlighted in each section. What shape you got the most of, or in some cases what combination of shapes you got, is going to tell you what your sensory pattern is for that sense.

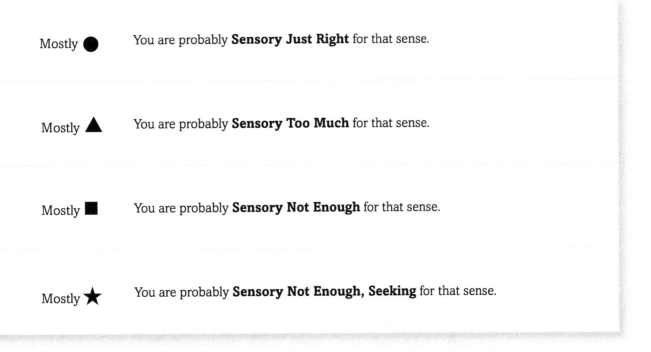

Mostly ● You are probably **Sensory Just Right** for that sense.

Mostly ▲ You are probably **Sensory Too Much** for that sense.

Mostly ■ You are probably **Sensory Not Enough** for that sense.

Mostly ★ You are probably **Sensory Not Enough, Seeking** for that sense.

What if you got a tie for some shapes? Or you got some of each shape? In that case, let's look at a few things …

- First, go back through your answers and make sure you paid attention to those words that talked about the frequency of a characteristic. You know, those words like "a lot," "often," or "not really." Do you need to change any of your answers and recalculate?

- Make sure that for the sets of boxes that instruct you to only choose the *one* statement that fits you best, you didn't accidentally choose more than one.

- When you have the results that tell you what sensory pattern you likely are, read the description (starting on page 88) and see if you think it describes you. The answers should make sense with what you experience on most days. For instance, if smells bother you a lot and you spend a lot of time avoiding them, then it would make sense that you are a "Too Much" for smell.

- If you have a mix of all of the shapes and have most of the circles, you might want to re-examine your answers and ask yourself if you are more of a "Just Right" for that sense and just experience occasional periods of other patterns. Remember, being "Just Right" doesn't mean always perfect.

- And sometimes, these sensory characteristics can just be really tricky. In that case, you might need to find a professional who can work directly with you to help you figure out exactly what your sensory patterns are. There is more info about finding a professional Sensory Expert who can work one-on-one with you at the end of the book.

# Workbook Section:
# Writing Down Your Sensory Patterns

It's time to officially record your sensory patterns! For each sense listed below, write down what pattern your questionnaire results gave.

| Senses | |
|---|---|
| Vision | |
| Hearing | |
| Taste | |
| Smell | |
| Touch | |
| Vestibular | |

# Patterns of Proprioception

Did you notice that there is not a section in the questionnaire for proprioception? No, I didn't forget it. The thing is, proprioception can be a little tricky,[3] so we are going to look at it differently. Here's the deal: proprioception just doesn't fit neatly into all of the modes, so we are not going to do a questionnaire that looks like the others. But we *can* talk about whether or not you are a Seeker for proprioception!

To do this, you will find a table below with a list of statements, a lot like what you saw in the Sensory Questionnaire. In this table, though, you will read each sentence and then decide if that statement describes things that you never do, sometimes do, or do all the time. Highlight the box with the shapes that fits you best, and we will add up your score at the end!

| | I never do this | I sometimes do this | I do this all the time! |
|---|---|---|---|
| I hold my pencil or pen very tightly when writing. | ◆ | ◖ | ♥ |
| I push down hard when I write or draw. Sometimes I break crayons or pencils because of this. | | | |
| When I close things like doors or drawers, I use too much force and slam them shut. | | | |
| When I give someone a hug, I squeeze really tight. | | | |
| I jump off things just to feel the landing. I might jump down the stairs, off my bed, or off the couch. | | | |
| Speaking of liking to jump down off things, I might do this over and over just to keep feeling it. | | | |
| I make piles of soft things, like cushions, pillow, and blankets, so that I can crash or fall into them. | | | |
| I stomp my feet when I walk or run. | | | |

| | |
|---|---|
| I bump into things, like a wall, on purpose. | |
| I love jumping on things like trampolines and want to jump for a very long time. | |
| I chew on things that are not food, like my shirt collar, a pen, or straws. | |
| TOTAL: | |

Time to tally up your results! Just like in the first Questionnaire, add up the number of shapes that you got for each shape. Then circle the shape that you got the most of.

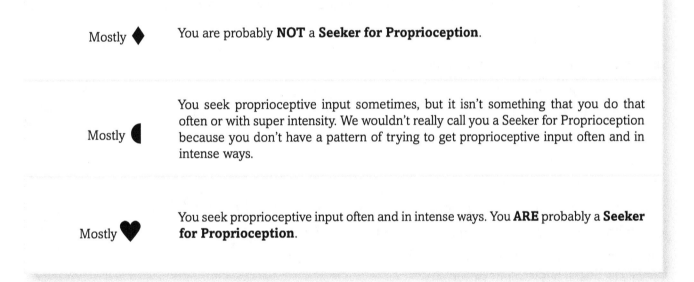

Mostly ◆  You are probably **NOT** a **Seeker for Proprioception**.

Mostly ◖  You seek proprioceptive input sometimes, but it isn't something that you do that often or with super intensity. We wouldn't really call you a Seeker for Proprioception because you don't have a pattern of trying to get proprioceptive input often and in intense ways.

Mostly ♥  You seek proprioceptive input often and in intense ways. You **ARE** probably a **Seeker for Proprioception**.

Again, just like for the Questionnaire results, if you aren't sure about your results after reading this, go back through your answers and check to see that you read each statement carefully and chose the best answer. Also, you can always find a Sensory Expert to provide that one-on-one support!

Oh, and if it turns out that you are a Seeker for proprioception, there are lots of ways to help your brain get the proprioceptive input that it wants! Keep reading, Exec.

# So, Exactly What Do My Sensory Patterns Look Like in Everyday Life?

All right, at this point you're a master at understanding how a brain takes in and understands sensory information. Also, you've taken the questionnaire, so you know about your own sensory patterns. What you know now looks something like this:

*"I am Sensory Too Much with vision, so my Brain Security Team lets in too much visual information and it does not screen that info for important stuff."*

*"I am Sensory Not Enough with hearing, so my Brain Security Team does not let in enough sound information, including the important stuff."*

*"I am Sensory Seeking with vestibular information, so my Brain Security Team does not let in enough movement info and my brain overrides into seeking mode, trying to find movement input."*

This is powerful information to know about yourself and a really important step in becoming a Brain Executive, but we want more detail. Remember, if an executive manages a pizza company, they'd better be an expert in pizza, right? We are talking not just "Pepperoni pizza is my favorite," but more "Pepperoni pizza is my favorite and the best pepperoni comes from a tiny shop in New York where they hand-make the pepperoni from scratch every day with a blend of pepper from three countries." Now that's knowing pepperoni. You see, what makes a really good executive is knowing the *details*.

Here is what it looks like when you know about your sensory patterns in detail:

*"I am Sensory Too Much with vision, so my Brain Security Team lets in too much visual information and it does not screen that info for important stuff. For me this means that I often get overwhelmed in places that have a lot to look at. In a classroom with a lot of stuff hanging on the wall and people moving around all the time, I have a really hard time focusing on what I am supposed to do. Also, bright lights bother me and sometimes give me a headache."*

*"I am Sensory Not Enough with hearing, so my Brain Security Team does not let in enough sound information, including the important stuff. For me that means that I don't always notice important sounds*

*like someone saying my name. Also, when a sound goes on and on without a lot of change it can be really hard for me to pay attention, like when my geography teacher talks for a super long time without stopping or changing his voice.”*

*“I am Sensory Seeking with vestibular information, so my Brain Security Team does not let in enough movement info and my brain overrides into seeking mode, trying to find movement input. For me this means that I have a really hard time sitting still and I usually squirm and fidget a lot. I also like to do fantastically intense movements like spinning super fast on a swing with my eyes closed.”*

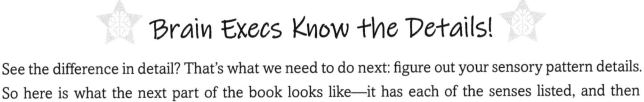

# Brain Execs Know the Details!

See the difference in detail? That's what we need to do next: figure out your sensory pattern details. So here is what the next part of the book looks like—it has each of the senses listed, and then for each sense it gives examples of how you might feel for each sensory pattern. That is a lot of information, but don't panic; you don't have to read it all! Here is what you do: look at your sensory pattern questionnaire results and find what pattern you are for each. Then read just that part for each sense. For example, if you are Sensory Too Much for vision, read that section, and you can skip the other parts for vision. And of course, if you want to read all the sections, go for it, Exec! The more you know, the better!

You should also know that if you read all of the sections, you will find some places where the same or similar statement is used in more than one mode. This is because things like having a difficult time focusing can happen in more than one mode.

One more thing before we get started. The lists of characteristics for each pattern are great for learning, but they do not provide examples of every possibility. That would be impossible, even for a Brain Exec. And you may not think that all of the characteristics listed in your mode are true about you. That is okay! The lists are simply examples of ways that a sensory mode might look for a certain sense. They are there to help you understand your sensory patterns better and to give you some examples of how you might experience them. There are definitely more ways that your patterns may show up every day, and once you get the idea from reading the lists, it's your job to think of how your own patterns work in your own life. At the end of each section is a page for you to record your own characteristics. Use whatever characteristics from the lists that fit you, but also try to think of your own. To do this, think through different parts of your day and consider how your senses are working.

## A Note for Adult Chief Advisors and Clinicians

Many of the statements listed in the Sensory Pattern Characteristic section can be the result of multiple factors and underlying causes, one of which is sensory modulation. These statements are not meant to be diagnostic indicators, but they can help the Brain Executive develop a better understanding of what sensory modulation challenges or well-being can look like in daily life.

# Sensory Pattern Characteristics

### Sense: Vision / Mode: Just Right

- The lighting in the room often seems to be just about right for what I need. This might mean that I am working with bright light to help me read or softer light while I relax before bedtime. It isn't that I have a specific amount of light—it's more about having the amount of light that fits what I want and what I am doing.

- I often seem to get a just-right amount of things to look at, so I don't feel overwhelmed and like there is too much to look at that often. I also don't feel bored because there isn't enough to look or like I want to try to see more. Once again, it isn't that I am getting any specific number of things to look at; it is that how much I am looking at fits what I want and need.

- Being in Just Right mode for vision helps me to do things like look at what I am doing, which also helps me to focus on the things that are important.

- Being in Just Right mode for vision also helps me to pick out the important things to look at. For instance, this may mean looking at my book when I am supposed to be reading or finding items on a search-and-find page. This is because my Brain Security Team is doing a good job at filtering the unimportant information.

- Even when I am in Just Right mode, sometimes I get distracted and look around at things other than what I am supposed to. When this happens, I usually notice and get back to paying attention pretty quickly.

## Sense: Vision / Mode: Too Much

- Lights often seem too bright to me.
- Bright lights bother me. This can be an inside light that is too bright or the sun when I am outside.
- I prefer soft colors like grays, tans, and pastels to bright colors like neon yellow or lime green.
- I notice if a light flickers and it is super annoying to me. Sometimes it gives me a headache.
- I feel overwhelmed and stressed out in places where I can see a lot of stuff all at once. This can be things like signs and pictures on the wall in a classroom or places like a busy store where there is a lot of stuff to look at and there are also people moving around.
- I have a hard time focusing on the words if I am reading a page that also has a lot of pictures or illustrations on it, especially if they are in bright colors.
- I dislike using highlighters because the neon color is way too bright.
- I don't like toys that have bright flashing lights.
- I also don't like watching toys that spin.
- I like for things to look organized, like a closet where all the clothes are in place instead of really messy and going everywhere all at once.
- I am easily distracted by things that I see.
- Sometimes I have a hard time ignoring things I can see around me, like the branches of a tree waving outside the window.
- I squint or cover my eyes a lot.
- Seeing bright, busy, crowded, and messy things can make me feel really stressed out or overwhelmed or even start a fight-or-flight response.

## Sense: Vision / Mode: Not Enough

- I don't really notice when my room or desk is messy.
- Sometimes I bump into things in my environment like a chair or wall. I just don't seem to notice them.
- Sometimes my friends are looking at something cool and I don't notice it.
- I don't always look at what I am supposed to. I feel like my eyes aren't good at paying attention to what is important.
- My teachers say that I write really messy, but I don't notice.
- My teachers also say that I don't leave enough space between letters and words when I write, or sometimes I leave too much. I don't notice these things either.
- I often lose my place on the page when I read because I have a hard time telling the important words that I am supposed to be focusing on from the other words.
- Sometimes I lose my place when I am reading because something that is not on the page (often something bright or moving) catches my attention. The black and white words just don't stand out enough to keep my attention.
- You know those pages and books that have hidden things in the picture for you to find? I have a really hard time with those because the stuff I am supposed to be looking for doesn't seem to stand out well in the middle of all of the other stuff.
- It takes me longer to complete assignments or tasks that involve seeing details like completing puzzles, doing math problems, organizing and cleaning up a space, and reading. I am just not always good at noticing details.
- People tell me to "pay attention" a lot.
- I can get distracted looking at the wrong stuff, especially if its bright, shiny, or moving.

## Sense: Vision / Mode: Seeking

- I love bright colors and busy patterns.
- I like watching TV most when the scene changes around a lot and moves fast. Sometimes I leave the TV on just to see the flashes of light.
- I like toys that have fast-moving parts such as spinners. I can watch them for a long time.
- Sometimes I make things move, like jiggling a pencil in my hand, just to watch the movement.
- If I am trying to read a book that has pictures and illustrations, I can "get lost" and look at the pictures more than the words, especially if the pictures and illustrations have bright colors. This can make it hard to read.
- Sometimes I bump into things in my environment like a chair or wall. I don't seem to notice them. Sometimes this happens because I am busy looking at something cool, like a fidget spinner in my hand.
- I prefer things that look messy and chaotic with lines and colors going everywhere. This makes stuff like math, where all the number are supposed to line up, really boring and sometimes hard to do.
- When I see something like a maze or a search-and-find page with tons of stuff on it, I like to look at it, but I am not always good at actually completing the maze or finding the stuff.
- It often takes me longer to complete assignments or tasks, sometimes because I don't notice all of the details but often because I get distracted looking around or looking at something really cool, like something that moves or is bright.
- People tell me to "pay attention" a lot.
- I like to put things really close to my eyes and look at them.

## Sense: Vision / My Mode:

Use the space here to write a list of characteristics you notice about your own sensory pattern for vision. You might use some of the examples listed on your pattern page, but don't forget that some of them probably don't fit you. Also, try to think of new ones! Thinking through a typical day is a great strategy.

## Sense: Hearing / Mode: Just Right

- Most of the time, the sounds where I am seem to be a just-right fit for what I need and want. For instance, if my friends have a movie playing and I join in, the sound usually seems okay. Or the way that most of my teachers talk seems to be a pretty good fit.

- I usually notice and can pay attention to the important stuff that people around me are saying.

- I can participate in groups where multiple people are talking. I am usually able to follow the important parts of the conversation, ask someone to talk louder if I can't hear, or be okay if the talking gets a bit loud at times.

- When I am in a place with loud noises I notice them, and sometimes they even bother me, but I am usually able to stay calm and keep doing whatever I am supposed to do.

- If people around me are talking too quietly or if the TV volume is too low, I notice and am generally able to solve the problem by listening closely, asking people to speak louder, or turning the volume up a little. This helps me to stay in Just Right mode.

- If I am in a busy environment with a lot of different sounds, I am usually able to pay attention to the sound that I am supposed to. For instance, during a busy field trip I can listen to my teacher giving directions.

## Sense: Hearing / Mode: Too Much

- When other people are listening to something like the TV or music, I often think that the volume is too loud.

- Background noise like music playing, a TV being on, or other people talking is super distracting to me. Working in groups when multiple people are talking is hard for me because all of the talking at once is overwhelming. Sometimes if one person has a high-pitched voice or a loud voice, their talking is all that I can pay attention to, even if what they are saying isn't important.

- Sometimes I have a hard time understanding and following directions because while the person telling me what to do is talking, other noises are bothering me or making me feel overwhelmed.

- Loud places like the lunchroom or a busy store really bother me. I feel overwhelmed in them, and sometimes I get anxious and can even have a fight or flight response.

- Noises that are sudden or unexpected really bother me and can often trigger a fight-or-flight response. If I am in a place where a sudden noise might happen, I am often on edge.

- I don't like playing music or the television loudly.

- I often hear noises that others don't notice, like humming of lights or the air conditioner running.

- I tell people to be quiet or to turn the volume down a lot.

- If I know that we are having a fire drill at school, I get really anxious waiting for the alarm to go off.

- If I am trying to focus on a task, I need the room to be quiet.

## Sense: Hearing / Mode: Not Enough

- When other people are listening to something like the TV or music, I sometimes think that the volume is not loud enough. Other times I don't really notice the volume, even though I don't really hear what is playing that well either.
- I don't always notice background noise like music playing, a TV being on, or other people talking.
- Working in groups when multiple people are talking is hard for me because I can't always figure out what the important stuff is to listen to, and sometimes I feel like everyone's voices just blend together.
- Sometimes I get in trouble for not following directions. It's not that I mean to not follow the directions; I just don't really hear them.
- Loud places like the lunchroom or a busy store don't really bother me, but sometimes I miss important stuff that is being said when there is other noise around.
- People tell me to "listen" and "pay attention" a lot.
- I don't always notice when people call my name.
- I seem to learn better in school when I am sitting up close to the teacher where I can hear the best.
- Sometimes people tell me I am talking too loudly, but I don't notice this at all.

## Sense: Hearing / Mode: Seeking

- When other people are listening to something like the TV or music, I often think that the volume is not loud enough. A lot of times I try to turn it up.
- I really like background noise like music playing, a TV being on, or other people talking. A lot of times I will put on background noise on purpose, like listening to music when I am doing my homework.
- Sometimes I get in trouble for not following directions. It's not that I mean to not follow the directions; I just don't really hear them. Sometimes when this happens, it is because I am focused on listening to a sound that I really like or maybe making sound myself.
- I love loud places like the lunchroom or a busy store. The louder the better!
- Sometimes playing loud music seems to calm me down.
- When I am in a situation that is too quiet for me, I make my own noise, like humming or tapping.
- In music class if we are playing instruments, I like to put mine right up next to my ear.
- People tell me to "pay attention "or "listen" all the time.
- I seem to learn better in school when I am sitting up close to the teacher where her voice sounds the loudest to me.

*So, hey, note from the author here: I totally get that you like to listen to loud things, but be careful. Really loud sounds can actually hurt your ears. Maybe pause here and have a conversation with your Chief Advisor about "Sound Safety."*

## Sense: Hearing / My Mode:

Use the space here to write a list of characteristics you notice about your own sensory pattern for hearing. You might use some of the examples listed on your pattern page, but don't forget that some of them probably don't fit you. Also, try to think of new ones! Thinking through a typical day is a great strategy.

## Sense: Taste / Mode: Just Right

- I am able to notice a variety of different flavors like sweet, sour, salty, and spicy.
- Being able to notice different flavors helps me know what foods I like and don't like.
- I have a lot of different foods that I like, and I will eat a variety of different things. This helps me to have a healthy diet.
- I might be a little picky about eating, but I am about the same amount of picky as most other kids my age.
- I can try new foods. It may not be my favorite thing to do, but I can usually try them without getting super upset or gagging. Actually, I sometimes find that I like the new foods that I try.
- Being able to notice differences in flavors also helps me to tell the difference between two foods without looking. For instance, if there are two kinds of chips to eat, one a ranch flavor and the other regular salt flavor, I can tell you which one I am eating with my eyes closed.

## Sense: Taste / Mode: Too Much

- I always notice the flavor of my food.
- I prefer foods that most people say are "plain" or "bland."
- I don't like a lot of spices on my food. Okay, to be honest I don't really like any.
- If I get a choice between a plain flavor like original salt chips or an intense flavor like extra spicy queso chips, I always choose the plain ones.
- In general, I will not try new foods. Honestly, it stresses me out to try new foods. I don't know how they might taste and make me feel.
- If I try to eat something that I don't like, it often makes me gag and feel like I am going to throw up.
- I am a very picky eater. With some foods I will only eat certain brands.
- I cannot always find something I like to eat at a restaurant or cafeteria. Sometimes I will skip the meal instead of eating something new or that I don't like.
- If I do try a new food, I take a tiny little bite of it first.

## Sense: Taste / Mode: Not Enough

- I don't really notice different flavors that much.
- Sometimes people say that a food tastes super sour, spicy, salty, or whatever, but I don't really notice it.
- I seem to be able to taste my food better when it has extra flavor.
- Sometimes I feel more awake after eating something with a strong flavor like sour candy or spicy salsa.
- Adults says that I am a "really good eater" because I will usually eat whatever they give me. The thing is, I don't notice the taste that much, so I don't care that much what I eat.

## Sense: Taste / Mode: Seeking

- I like really strong and intense flavors.
- People think I am weird for liking such strong flavors, but I just do. Super-sour candy? Yes! Salt and vinegar chips? You bet! Five-alarm spicy salsa? I want it all!
- I like adding stuff, like salt or spices, to my food. I add a lot of them.
- Sometimes I feel more awake after eating something with a strong flavor like sour candy or spicy salsa.
- Sometimes I like to taste things that aren't food. I just really like to see what things taste like.
- Sometimes I seem to pay better attention if I can chew gum with a strong flavor, like intense mint or spicy cinnamon.
- I like to try new foods. I enjoy the way that the new flavors surprise you.

*Hi again, note from the author here: I totally get that you like to taste different things, but be careful. Not everything is safe to taste. Maybe pause here and have a conversation with your Chief Advisor about what might not be safe to taste.*

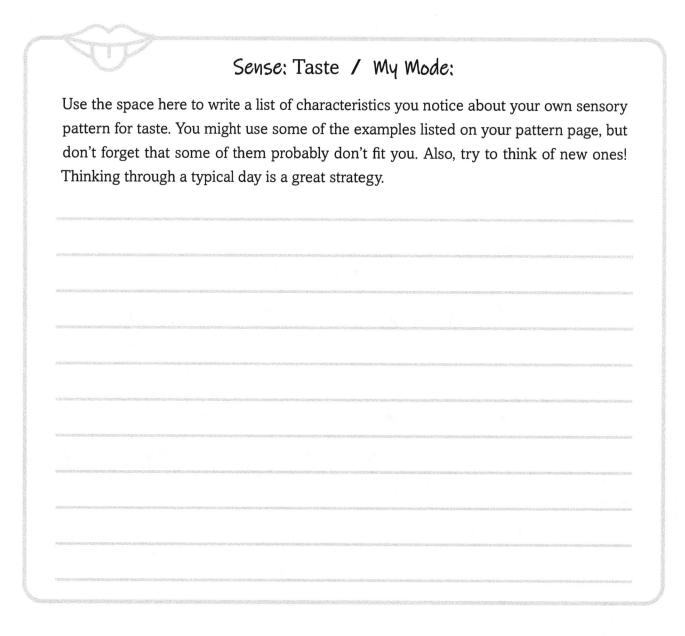

## Sense: Taste / My Mode:

Use the space here to write a list of characteristics you notice about your own sensory pattern for taste. You might use some of the examples listed on your pattern page, but don't forget that some of them probably don't fit you. Also, try to think of new ones! Thinking through a typical day is a great strategy.

## Sense: Smell  /  Mode: Just Right

- In general, I smell things that most other people do. Like if someone notices a stinky smell from the trash, so do I. Or if Grandma just started baking and my sister notices the amazing smell of her sugar cookies, I notice it too.

- I can notice a smell that I don't like, and even though it might bother me a little, I can usually keep doing whatever I need to.

- If there is a *really* bad smell, I might gag, but usually I can smell something that I dislike without actually feeling like I am going to throw up.

- I can list quite a few things that I like or dislike the smell of. For instance, I like the smell of cinnamon, vanilla, oranges, cakes baking, and my first-grade teacher's perfume. I do not like the smell of trash, fish, my hamster's cage, or when I have to walk my dog and he, well, you know …

- I enjoy smelling things like scented candles or different perfumes, but after taking a few good smells of them, I am good and generally don't need to continue smelling them forever.

- Since I seem to get a just-right amount of sensory info from my nose, I can often use smell to tell me about something. Like if you blindfold me and let me smell a hamburger versus a piece of pizza, I could tell you which was which.

## Sense: Smell / Mode: Too Much

- I often smell things that other people don't notice.
- A lot of times I smell something before others do. For instance, I am always the first to notice when the trash starts to stink and needs to be taken out.
- I seem to smell things more than other people do. Like if a teacher is wearing a perfume or cologne that my friend may notice but forget, all I can think about when that teacher is near is how much their cologne smells.
- Sometimes a certain smell will really bother me and I want to get away from it. That teacher in the last example? She is really nice, but I avoid being close to her as much as possible. I would rather try to figure out a math problem myself than call her over and have to smell her perfume.
- Smells often make me gag or feel like I might throw up, even when other people don't think the smell is that bad.
- If I am asked to smell something, I try to smell it from a really long way away. I definitely don't want to put my nose right next to something to smell.
- I avoid going places that have strong smells, like the lunchroom or public bathrooms.
- The smell of cleaning supplies and detergents really bothers me.
- I complain about smells more than others do.

## Sense: Smell / Mode: Not Enough

- I don't really notice smells that much.
- Sometimes everyone is talking about how bad something smells and I just don't notice it. Even when I try to smell it, I don't really think it's that bad.
- Since I am not really great at getting enough information about smells, I sometimes find it hard to tell the difference between smells.
- I seem to feel more awake if there is a strong smell in the air. One of my teachers has a really minty peppermint oil diffuser in the classroom, and I think I learn better when it's on.
- You know how you are supposed to be able to smell milk to see if it has gone bad? I smelled some right out of the carton the other day and thought it was fine, so I put it on my cereal. When my sister smelled it, she gagged and almost threw up because she said it was so sour. I tried to smell it again, but I still didn't notice.

## Sense: Smell / Mode: Seeking

- I love to smell different things.
- I really like stuff that other people think smells too strongly. Our math teacher wears a lot of cologne and it bothers my friends but I think it smells really good. One day I snuck over to his desk to smell it straight from the bottle.
- I like to put things right up to my nose to smell them so that I get the strongest smell.
- Sometimes I will hold things up to my nose and smell them for a long time. I just can't get enough.
- When other people smell something they might just take a small sniff, I take a big, deep breath and enjoy the smell.
- I know everyone complains about places that smell a lot, like the lunchroom, but I really like them.
- I find things around me to smell, especially when I am bored. At my desk sometimes I smell my notebook, my pencils, or my shirt sleeve.

*So, hey, note from the author here: I totally get that you like to smell things, but be careful. Not everything is safe to smell. Maybe pause here and have a conversation with your Chief Advisor about "Smell Safety."*

## Sense: Smell / My Mode:

Use the space here to write a list of characteristics you notice about your own sensory pattern for smell. You might use some of the examples listed on your pattern page, but don't forget that some of them probably don't fit you. Also, try to think of new ones! Thinking through a typical day is a great strategy.

## Sense: Touch / Mode: Just Right

- In general, I can engage in activities like cooking or art projects that involve something that gets on my hands and fingers and can feel kind of messy. I notice the mess and how it feels, but it doesn't bother me too much.

- If something messy gets on my hands, face, or body while I eat or work, I notice, do my best to clean it off, and keep working, playing, or eating.

- I am okay with feeling different textures and surfaces. Some of them I like and some of them I don't, but even when I don't like them, it doesn't bother me that much.

- I notice when someone taps me on the arm or shoulder to get my attention, but it doesn't usually startle me.

- If someone bumps into me or brushes up against me, I notice but it doesn't usually bother me that much. I am able to do something like move out of the way and keep working or playing.

- I notice the feel of my clothes. I definitely have some favorites because of how soft the fabric is or how comfortable the clothing feels, but I can wear clothes that aren't my favorite and be okay.

- Sometimes things like seams or tags in clothing bother me, but in general I can ignore them most of the time.

- If my clothing is crooked, like a sleeve twisted, I usually notice and I am able to fix it.

- I am okay with things like brushing my teeth and hair or getting my nails trimmed.

- Sometimes I like to feel different items, like fabric or a bumpy surface, but I don't need to do it all the time without stopping. I seem to like it about as much as others do.

## Sense: Touch / Mode: Too Much

- There are some textures, fabrics, or surfaces that I really don't like and will strongly avoid touching. Things like velvet or fleece might feel icky to touch and can even cause me to feel stress or anxiety.
- It really, really dislike "messy play," or things that are supposed to be fun, but involve something that is messy. This can include things like fingerpainting, using modeling clay, or cooking.
- If I have to touch something that I don't like the feel of, I use just the tip of one finger and touch whatever it is a quickly and as little as I can.
- It really bothers me if someone accidentally bumps into me or brushes up against me. In situations when this might happen, like standing in line, I might feel anxious. Also, if this happens, it can really startle me and can kick off a fight-or-flight response in which I jump away really fast or maybe do something like push or yell. It's not that I mean to get mad or hurt anyone; I just feel alarmed.
- The feel of clothing can really bother me. Something like a tag in a shirt or a seam can itch, scratch, or hurt and I can't stop feeling it and paying attention to it. It makes it hard to pay attention to other things.
- Parts of my clothing often feel too tight, so I keep pulling on it to try to situate it better.
- I will only wear a few different items of clothing, and I wear them all the time because they feel okay.
- I really dislike things such as brushing my teeth and hair or having my nails trimmed. I avoid them and sometimes argue a lot when it is time to do them.
- Some foods I won't eat not because of taste, but because of how they feel and their texture.

## Sense: Touch / Mode: Not Enough

- I have no problems engaging in messy projects like fingerpainting, modeling with clay, or cooking. If I notice that stuff gets on me, it doesn't bother me, but honestly a lot of the times I don't even notice it.

- I don't usually notice different kinds of fabrics or how they feel different. For instance, I never think about which of my clothes or blankets feel soft or itchy; I just use them.

- I don't notice if the clothes I am wearing get twisted around on my body.

- Sometimes when I eat or play, I get stuff on my face or hands and I don't notice it.

- People often have to tell me to wipe my face.

- I often don't notice if anyone bumps into me or brushes against me. If I do, it doesn't bother me at all.

- A lot of times I don't notice if someone taps me on the shoulder or arm to try to get my attention.

- You know how some people can do things like button a button, zip a zipper, or maybe put on their socks without really looking? Not me. I don't really feel the button, zipper, or sock that well, so I need to be looking to know what to do.

- You know how some people can reach into their backpack to fish out a pencil without looking? Not me. I try but I just don't seem to be getting enough feeling from my fingers, so eventually I just have to look.

# Sense: Touch / Mode: Seeking

- I love being in busy places where people might bump up against me.
- I bump and rub up against things on purpose to feel them. I am often the kid who walks down the hallway with their arm or hand on the wall.
- If I am supposed to stand still, I prefer to lean up against something like a wall or a desk. It's not that I am tired; I just like the feel.
- I love feeling different things. I can run my fingers over a fabric or surface forever. I like to feel the difference between something scratchy like sandpaper or smooth like satin.
- I have some items that I have worn out because I touch and rub them so much. Rubbing and fidgeting with them over and over causes places to be worn thin in objects like blankets, pillows, rugs, or whatever else I like the feel of.
- I like to fidget with things in my hands. I do this more than others do.
- Adults often tell me to "stop touching everything."
- I love doing things that are messy like cooking or art projects that involve stuff like fingerpainting or modeling clay. The sticky/slimy feeling is the best.
- When other people are touching something new with just a finger, I jump in and grab it with my whole hand. I want to feel it all!

## Sense: Touch / My Mode:

Use the space here to write a list of characteristics you notice about your own sensory pattern for touch. You might use some of the examples listed on your pattern page, but don't forget that some of them probably don't fit you. Also, try to think of new ones! Thinking through a typical day is a great strategy.

# Sense: Vestibular / Mode: Just Right

- I seem to want to move around about as much as other kids my age.
- The amount of movement that I get most days seems to fit what I need.
- I am comfortable doing movements like spinning, jumping, and running.
- Sometimes I like doing fast, intense movements, but when I am supposed to move slowly, like walking in the hallways at school, I can.
- Sure, sometimes I stumble or maybe even fall, but I don't seem to do so more than others.
- I am pretty good at climbing.
- Sometimes heights might scare me, especially if they are really high up, but I wouldn't say that I am scared of heights in general.
- I enjoy doing things like swinging or riding a carousel.
- I can keep my balance, even with my eyes closed.
- I am able to do things like riding a bike or skateboard without feeling extra scared that my feet are not on the ground.

## Sense: Vestibular / Mode: Too Much

- I don't like fast movement. I prefer to move slowly. When I move slowly, I feel like I am more in control and less likely to have any unexpected movement like stumbling or falling.
- I often prefer activities that don't require movement, like reading or watching TV.
- I specifically do not like movements like moving backwards, spinning, or swinging. They make me feel unstable, unsteady, fearful, and sometimes sick.
- Sometimes movements make me feel fearful and can even start a fight-or-flight response.
- I really dislike heights. Even low heights are scary.
- I dislike things like low balance beams or trying to walk down the curb on a street. I prefer my feet to be on solid ground.
- I don't like the feeling of tipping my head back. It makes me feel unsteady and uncertain. Washing the soap out of my hair in the shower is a problem because of this.
- I don't like riding on things like bikes or skateboards. They feel tippy and unstable and can make me feel really fearful. I prefer my feet to be on the ground.
- I often get motion sickness. This includes riding in cars, buses, and planes, and things like carousels, see-saws, or swings.
- Did I mention that I don't like to swing?
- You know those escalating steps in airports and malls? The ones where you stand still but the stairs move? Those make me feel sick and unsteady. Same thing with elevators. I prefer regular stairs.
- Closing my eyes makes me feel very off-balance and sometimes queasy.

## Sense: Vestibular / Mode: Not Enough

- I rarely get motion sickness or feel uneasy because of motion.
- I can spin forever and not really seem to feel dizzy.
- I seem to stumble and fall more than others. It's just that I don't always seem to get where my body is or how it is moving.
- I have a hard time staying alert and focused when I am supposed to be sitting for a while, like in class.
- I seem to feel the most alert and focused after I move around a lot. This is especially true if I move in ways that are intense like spinning or running around with a lot of changes in directions and stopping.
- I have a really hard time keeping my balance if I close my eyes.
- Doing things that require balance, like walking across a balance beam or riding a bike, seems to be especially hard for me.

# Sense: Vestibular / Mode: Seeking

- I love to move, and I prefer activities that involve a lot of movement.
- People describe me as "always on the go."
- I typically move fast when possible. I am a "run, don't walk" kind of person.
- I love intense actions like spinning, swinging, and climbing.
- When I am performing movements, I try to make them more intense. For instance, if I am spinning, I try to spin really fast or for a long time. If I am swinging, I try to swing as high as I can.
- I can spin for a long time and not feel dizzy.
- I like to do things like crashing and falling on purpose.
- Peoples sometimes think that I am a "daredevil" because I like to do things like jumping off a high step or riding my skateboard as fast as I can.
- People tell me to slow down a lot.
- I have a hard time sitting still. I fidget a lot when I have to.
- If I am not moving, I have a hard time paying attention.

*So, hey, note from the author here: I totally get that those fast and intense kinds of movements feel good, and we will have safe strategies in the next part of the book to help you get vestibular info to your brain, but also, could you please be careful? Maybe pause here and have a conversation with your Chief Advisor about safety.*

## Sense: Vestibular / My Mode:

Use the space here to write a list of characteristics you notice about your own sensory pattern for vestibular. You might use some of the examples listed on your pattern page, but don't forget that some of them probably don't fit you. Also, try to think of new ones! Thinking through a typical day is a great strategy.

## Sense: Proprioception / Mode: Seeking

- Sometimes I do things like flinging my arm or legs around just because it feels good.
- I like to stretch and push my joints to the end of where they go. Some people think that stretching hurts, but I think it feels good.
- I like to crash and fall into things; it just feels so great. Sometimes I get in trouble for doing things like jumping down off the couch or falling down on a trampoline on purpose.
- I often arrange something soft like cushions and blankets so that I can crash into them.
- Speaking of trampolines, I love them. I could jump on them forever.
- I really like to chew on things. Sometimes I chew things like my clothing or straws. I also like chewy food and gum. *(Hey, Exec, did you know that you get proprioceptive information from the muscles and joints in your mouth and jaw when you chew?!)*
- I often use too much force when I do things. I give really tight hugs. I need reminders to be gentle when playing with babies and young kids. I squeeze my pencil really tightly.
- I push down really hard when I write, which mean I break a lot of pencil leads and crayons.

*So, hey, note from the author here: I totally get that those hard and intense kinds of movements like crashing feel good, and we will have safe strategies in the next part of the book to help you get vestibular info to your brain, but also, could you please be careful? Maybe pause here and have a conversation with your Chief Advisor about safety.*

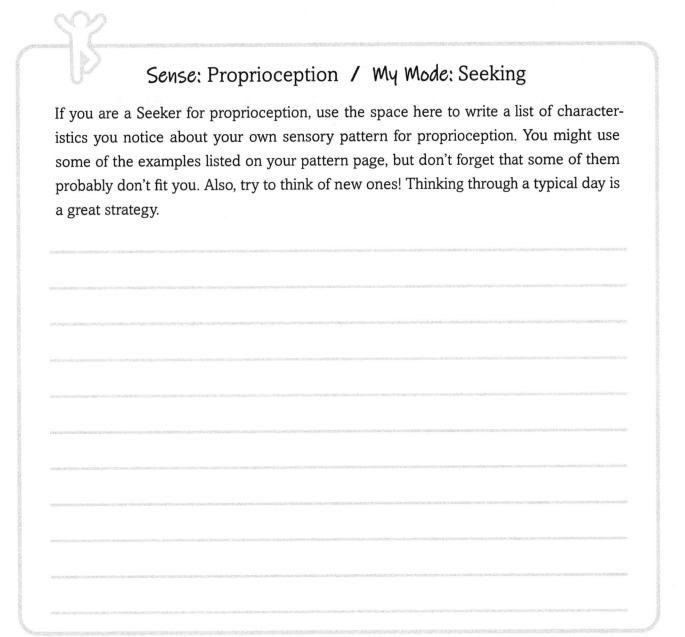

## Sense: Proprioception / My Mode: Seeking

If you are a Seeker for proprioception, use the space here to write a list of characteristics you notice about your own sensory pattern for proprioception. You might use some of the examples listed on your pattern page, but don't forget that some of them probably don't fit you. Also, try to think of new ones! Thinking through a typical day is a great strategy.

# Workbook Section:
# Brain Exec Activity – Sensory Diary

Remember what I said about how important it is to know your Sensory Pattern details? Well, I am going to say it again, because it really is super important!

## "It is important to know your Sensory Pattern details!"

Since it is so important, let's look at it in another way. On the next pages are blank entries for a Sensory Diary. This is not the kind of diary where you write all your secrets. In this diary you are going to really think about your sensory systems working in everyday situations.

On the top lines you are going to describe a typical situation for you. This could be something like math class, gym, baseball after school, watching TV at home, or playing with your little bro. Just think of things that you do every day.

Then, in the boxes below, describe what each of your senses is doing during this activity. Write down what info they are taking in and what modes you are typically in. If you can think of ways that your brain security team is taking in too much or not enough info, or ways that you are seeking more sensory input during the activity, definitely write that down!

Visit **brainexecutiveprogram.com** to download additional Sensory Diary Worksheets.

## Brain Exec Activity – Sensory Diary Worksheet

Describe the situation:

_____

_____

_____

Vision

Hearing

Taste

Smell

Touch

Vestibular

Proprioception

## Brain Exec Activity – Sensory Diary Worksheet

Describe the situation:

_____

_____

_____

Vision

Hearing

Taste

Smell

Touch

Vestibular

Proprioception

## Brain Exec Activity – Sensory Diary Worksheet

Describe the situation:

_____

_____

_____

Vision

Hearing

Taste

Smell

Touch

Vestibular

Proprioception

## Brain Exec Activity – Sensory Diary Worksheet

Describe the situation:

_____

_____

_____

Vision

Hearing

Taste

Smell

Touch

Vestibular

Proprioception

## Brain Exec Activity – Sensory Diary Worksheet

Describe the situation:

_____

_____

_____

Vision

Hearing

Taste

Smell

Touch

Vestibular

Proprioception

# Managing Sensory Modes and Patterns

# Can We Get to the Part Where We Help Our Brain?

Guess what? It's the moment you've been waiting for! (Could we get a drum roll again, please?) Now that you understand sensory modulation and your own sensory patterns, we can learn how to actually *help your brain* move more toward Just Right mode. That's a big statement, so let me say it again in Brain Exec terms: we are going to use our brainy knowledge to help our security teams block out or let in sensory input, so that our brains get more of a just-right amount.

Think of a thermometer. Let's say that this thermometer is in a pot of soup that you are cooking on the stove. It can tell you how hot or cold the soup is, which helps you know if it is cooking right.

So let's say that we need this pretend soup that we are cooking to be "simmering." Not too hot so that it is boiling, but hot enough so that it will cook.

The middle of the thermometer is "Just Right Temperature." When the soup is at this temperature, it is simmering, bubbling just a little, cooking, and smelling amazing.

The right side of the thermometer is "Too Hot." If the soup reaches this temperature, it will start boiling too much, maybe boil over, and even burn. That sounds like a mess. And, no thanks to eating burnt soup.

On the other hand, the left side of the thermometer is "Not Hot Enough." If your soup is at a temperature in this area, it won't be hot enough to cook. No bubbling, no yummy smells. In fact, that soup is still raw. Yuck.

So what do you do if you are cooking soup and the thermometer is showing that the temperature is too hot or too cold? Let's take a quiz and see if you know. Don't panic; it's only two questions.

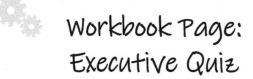

# Workbook Page: Executive Quiz

Think about what is going on in each scenario and choose the best answer.

1. You are cooking the Best Chicken Noodle Soup Ever. (You know this because when you looked up the recipe, it is literally named "The Best Chicken Noodle Soup Ever.") The thing is, the temperature isn't hot enough, so the soup is not cooking. What can you do to move the thermometer toward Just Right Temperature?
   a. Turn the heat up until the soup starts bubbling
   b. Turn the heat down
   c. Turn the heat all the way off and let the soup cool
   d. Both b and c

2. You are cooking the same Best Chicken Noodle Soup Ever, but this time the temperature is too hot. It keeps boiling over the sides of the pot, and you start to smell something burning. What can you do to move the thermometer toward Just Right Temperature?
   a. Turn the heat up some
   b. Turn the heat down
   c. Turn the heat all the way off and let the soup cool
   d. Both b and c

Did you pass the quiz and are ready to be a professional chef? Sounds great! Okay, but wait. How does this all relate to sensory stuff? Good question. Let me explain …

I like to think of the sensory modes on a meter, also. It helps me see if my Brain Security Team is letting in too much or not enough information, just like a thermometer helps me know if I am using too much or not enough heat.

In my imagination, my Sensory Meter looks something like this:

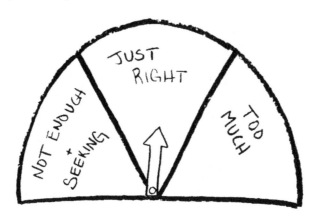

The middle of the meter is Just Right—this indicates that you are in Just Right mode. The amount of sensory information getting up to your brain is a just-right fit for whatever you are doing.

On the right side of your meter is Too Much mode. When the needle of your meter is pointing here, your brain security team is letting in too much sensory info and your brain is getting overwhelmed. You know what this looks like: having a hard time paying attention to what is important, feeling distracted, maybe feeling anxious, wanting to get away, perhaps being in Fight or Flight mode.

The left side of your meter is Not Enough mode and Not Enough, Seeking mode. If the needle of your Sensory Meter is pointing here, your brain security team is not letting in enough information. You know what this looks like too. You might be lethargic, drowsy, bored, or "checked out," or you might be super active, trying to seek out more sensory information. Either way, you are having a hard time paying attention to the important stuff and might feel distracted.

# Moving the Needle on Our Sensory Meter

With all the information that you have learned, you are probably getting pretty good at reading your Sensory Meter. You also know that when you are in Just Right mode, you can work at your best, because your brain is getting a Just Right amount of sensory information. So the big question here is:

**If we are in Sensory Too Much mode, Sensory Not Enough mode, or Sensory Not Enough, Seeking mode, can we help our brains move toward Just Right mode?**

The answer is:

So how do we move our Sensory Meter toward a Just Right mode? It is all about helping your Brain Security Team, my friend! What is that? Oh, you want to know how to help your security team? Here are some options.

Option 1: Open up your brain and go in to help the security team.

Ummm, I am going to go with a no for that one. Sounds like it might hurt.

Option 2: Shout out directions to your security team. Like this: "Hey, security team! You need to let in more sound!"

No again on this one, Exec, because that is not using good brain language. Go ahead and try if you want. Shout those sentences out in the room wherever you are and see if it makes a difference. [dramatic pause] If you actually tried that, or even just imagined it, you probably figured out that it didn't work. Like we said in the beginning of this book, your brain needs to be communicated with in Brain Language, and this does not involve just shouting things at it.

So then, how exactly do we help our security team either block out or get more sensory information? Let me share Option 3. (Hint: this is the right option.)

Option 3: Make changes in the environment around you or the activity that you are doing in ways that sends either more or less information to your Brain Security Team.

You can help your security team out by making a few changes in the things around you or in whatever activity you are doing.[5,10,13,17] Small changes like wearing noise-canceling headphones can make a big difference by blocking out sounds for a Too Much. On the other hand, if you are a Not Enough or a Seeker, a change like sitting closer to whoever is talking can help to give your brain more sound. Let's look at a few examples of this idea using vision to give you a better idea of how it works.

# Executive Example – Sensory Too Much

Let's say that you are in class, learning about how a monkey named Albert was the first primate to travel in space. (I'm for real; it's a true story.)

You are in Sensory Too Much mode for vision, so the needle of your Sensory Meter is over to the right side. What can you do to help your Brain Security Team block out sensory input and bring the needle toward Just Right?

Sometimes changing where you are in a room can help. For instance, if you are sitting at the back of the room and looking toward the teacher, there is a ton of stuff to see between you and them. On the other hand, if you are sitting on the front row in class, your teacher is probably directly in front of you, so there isn't as much to see between you and them. Less stuff to see means less visual info for your brain, helping you move more toward Just Right.

Or maybe there is something specific that bothers you, like flickering fluorescent lights in the room. To move your meter toward Just Right, we need to get rid of the flickering light, but you can't just sit in a dark classroom all the time. No problem. You can work with your teacher to turn off the overhead lights and use lamps in the room instead. (Lamps use bulbs that aren't fluorescent, so they don't do that annoying flickering thing.) In this case, instead of having fewer things to see, we are giving your brain less intense things to see. Same idea, though: we are sending less input to your brain, so we are moving your meter toward Just Right.

Like these examples of how to move your Sensory Meter and want more? Don't worry, the next part of the book is filled with them!

# Executive Example –
# Sensory Not Enough and Seeking

Let's keep going with this example: same class, same learning about Albert flying into space. But this time, let's say that you are in Not Enough mode or Not Enough, Seeking mode for vision. This means that you are on the left side of your Sensory Meter. To move toward Just Right mode, you need to add *more* visual input. How can you do that in class?

Changing your position in the room can also help when you need more visual input. If you are in the back of the classroom, your teacher is kinda far away and sort of small. So is all the stuff on the board that you are supposed to be looking at. Moving to the front brings you closer to your teacher and the board, making them bigger and right there in front of you. Bigger and closer things give more input to the brain, which helps move your needle toward Just Right. Also, notice that you are getting more of the *important* stuff, not just more visual input in general.

Using a strategy that I call "spotlighting" can also help move a Not Enough or a Seeker toward Just Right. Have you ever been to a play or concert where the room is sort of dark but they use a bright spotlight to highlight one actor or singer? What is everyone looking at? The person in the spotlight, right?! We can use this strategy in the classroom too. I mean, not exactly a spotlight, but the teacher can turn the lights off in the back of the classroom and keep the lights on in the front of the room, where they are teaching. They can even point some bright lamps toward them. All of this brightness adds more visual information up near the teacher, helping you move toward Just Right!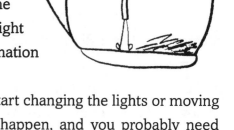

(Executive Advice: Talk to the adults in charge before you start changing the lights or moving your seat! They can be super helpful in making these things happen, and you probably need permission.)

Can't wait to learn more strategies? Like I said, there are more to come in the next pages!

Do you see how we can work to move the needle on your Sensory Meter toward Just Right by using strategies that either give your brain more or less sensory information? You are helping your security team out by sending more info to a Not Enough or Seeking team and sending less info to a Too Much team. And, since security teams in these modes don't do a great job of screening for important information, our strategies help them do this as well. How? Just like in the examples that you just read, the strategies help to block out unimportant information and highlight the important stuff.

Now that you have the basic idea, I am going to give examples to use for each of your senses. But first, there is a bit of information that you need to know …

☑ Brain Fact: *Did you notice that I keep saying "toward Just Right mode" instead of always saying "into Just Right mode"? Here's the thing: your brain doesn't have to be perfect to be great. In fact, what is perfect anyway??? My point being, don't think that your goal has to be to always be in Just Right mode. No one is always in Just Right mode, and besides, don't forget that there are good things and challenges for every mode. BUT if you are experiencing the challenges of Too Much, Not Enough, or Seeking modes, and they are getting in the way of you doing awesome things, it's safe to say that we would like to help you move more toward a Just Right state.*

Sometimes you will be able to move the arrow on your Sensory Meter all the way into Just Right. Great! Other times you will be able to move the arrow closer to Just Right, but maybe not all the way. Also great! Let's say that you are a Too Much and your Sensory Meter is reading *way* over to the right. You are feeling overwhelmed, super anxious, and in fight-or-flight. But then you think, "I'm a Brain Exec! I know my security team is having a hard time blocking out information right now, but it's okay, I can help!" So you use some brainy strategies and the needle on your Sensory Meter starts moving left, toward Just Right. Maybe it gets *almost* to Just Right, but then stops and hangs out it "a little Too Much" zone. The good news is, you might still be feeling a little overwhelmed, but in "a little Too Much" zone you aren't in fight-or-flight and you aren't feeling super anxious. Even if there is a little too much info going to your brain, you can keep on doing whatever it is that you want or need to do. And that is the point, right, Exec?

# Workbook Section:
# Brain Exec Activity – Make Your Own Sensory Meter

This Sensory Meter idea is pretty important, and looking at the drawings of it is good, but making one so that you can actually move the arrow on your meter is top-notch learning! Here's what to do:

What you need: white construction paper, scissors, a pencil, markers or colored pencils, something called a "brad" (As in office supplies brad, not a person Brad. You are going to use it to hold your meter together so it seems like a small piece of metal is the way to go, not an actual person.)

Cut out a half-circle in your construction paper. Then, using your markers or colored pencils, divide it into thirds like this:

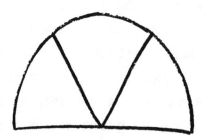

Write "Just Right" in the center, "Too Much" on the right, and "Not Enough + Seeking" on the left. Then cut an arrow out of the left-over paper, and using the brad, attach it to the bottom of your Sensory Meter at the center. Voila! Not you can move the arrow on your meter to show your sensory mode.

# Strategies for Helping Your Brain Security Team

Next up are lists of strategies to help your Brain Security Team bring you closer to Just Right mode. These strategies are organized by senses. For each sense there will be one list for Too Muches, with ways to help your team block out or get less sensory input, and another list for Not Enoughs and Seekers to help your team get more sensory input. A couple of things that you need to know:

For starters, you only have to read the parts that apply to you. Just like those lists of sensory pattern characteristics, you get to flip through the pages and only read the ones that help you and your patterns.

Also, similar to those lists of sensory pattern characteristics, these lists are not complete lists of every possible strategy you can use to help your Brain Security Team. Once again, that would be impossible, even for a Brain Exec. These lists for sure give you ideas that you can use, but the bigger point is to get you thinking about how you can help your team out. Once you get the idea, you can make up your own strategies!

Oh, and when you are using these strategies, you should probably often ask the adults in charge if they are okay to do. I am all about doing things that help you be a better you, but we have to follow the rules and be respectful of others. Don't forget: everyone around you is in their own sensory mode and we don't want to change things that would make it harder for them.

Ready?

## Executive Strategies – Vision, Too Much

- Change your position in the room so that there is less stuff to look at between you and whatever you are doing. In the classroom, this might mean sitting in the front row to be close to the teacher.
- Change your position in the room so that you are not close to a place where there are new things to look at all the time. This might mean not sitting close to a door that has a window to the hallway so that you are always watching people walk down the hall or moving away from a window where there are cars driving past.
- Wear sunglasses or a hat to block out the sun when it is too bright.
- Turn down the lights in a room or turn some of them off.
- Use lamps instead of overhead lights.
- Use incandescent lights instead of fluorescent ones.
- Use blank sheets of paper to block out parts of a page so that only a little shows at a time.
- Use pastel markers for highlighting instead of neon highlighters.
- Keep rooms and areas where you work organized.
- When choosing colors, try to use soft, pastels, or neutrals instead of bright or neon ones.
- Change the position of your desk so that it faces a blank wall.
- Use a Vision Break—periodically close your eyes and let your eyes and brain rest for a minute.
- Create a cubicle at your work station—use folders or cardboard shields to go on your desk that block you from seeing around the room.
- Remove brightly colored rugs and decorations or stuff with patterns.

# Executive Strategies – Vision, Not Enough + Seeking

- Change position in the room so that you are closer to whatever you are supposed to be paying attention to. In the classroom, this might mean sitting in the front row to be close to the teacher.
- Change position in the room so you are not close to stuff that is distracting like a hallway where people walk by or a window.
- Turn the lights on brightly where you are working.
- Use bright colors when writing. (You might have to ask your teacher if it is okay to use colored pens and explain to them why it helps.)
- You know how some brands of notebook paper have pale blue and red lines but other brands have darker, bolder blue and red? Go shopping for the ones with darker, bolder colors to help you notice the lines.
- Use reading strip highlighters to bring your attention to the words that you are reading on a page. (Don't know what these are? They are small strips with "windows" in to show the words that you are reading.)
- Use graph paper for math to help you line up the numbers correctly.
- Turn off the TV when you are working; the bright flashes of light will be very tempting to look at.
- Use a bright colored mat on your desk to place your papers on.
- Create a cubicle at your workstation—use folders or cardboard shields to go on your desk so that you cannot see distracting stuff around the room.
- Color code supplies to make them easy to find.
- Remove "clutter" from the room so there are less distractions.

My Executive Strategies - Vision

My Mode: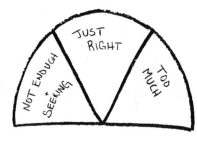

Draw an arrow on the Sensory Meter showing where your mode typically is for **vision**. Then use the space below to write down some ideas for strategies to help your Brain Security Team out. You can use some examples that are given in the book, but also try to think of new ones!

# Executive Strategies – Hearing, Too Much

- Change positions in the room so that you are close to the important source of noise, like sitting near the teacher of the TV.
- Change positions in the room so that you are not close to a distracting source of noise. This might mean moving away from a window where you can hear people outside or moving away from a refrigerator whose motor is running.
- Use noise-canceling headphones or hearing-protection earplugs. (When shopping for earplugs, you can look for ones that are small and skin colored if you don't want other people to notice them. Also, you need to ask an adult to help you learn to put them in and take them out safely.)
- Use a fan or white noise app to help block out other sounds.
- Ask an adult to warn you when there might be unexpected or loud noises. Like asking a grown up to remind you that there might be banging from a construction zone when you walk by or asking your teacher to let you know that there will be a fire drill today.
- Ask for breaks when you are working in a loud environment.
- When doing group work, implement talking rules so that only one person is talking at a time.
- When doing focused work, try to turn off any noise-makers in the room, like a radio or TV.
- Talk to your teachers at school about having a quiet environment to work in when you are doing focused work like testing.
- When in a busy environment, ask for directions in writing.
- Spend time reviewing the plan for responding to alarms like the fire alarm so when the loud sound happens you are more likely to remember what to do.

## Executive Strategies – Hearing, Not Enough + Seeking

- Change positions in the room so that you are close to the important source of noise, like sitting near the teacher of the TV.

- Change positions in the room so that you are not near a distracting source of noise. This might mean moving away from a window where you can hear people outside or moving away from a friend who likes to talk.

- Use your vision to help your hearing. How? Do things like looking at whoever is talking or using written directions in addition to spoken directions.

- If you are around someone who is speaking quietly, politely ask them to speak up.

- You can also ask someone to speak more slowly so that each sound makes more sense.

- If your teacher is going to be talking for a while, ask them to change their voice every now and then to help you pay attention. Some changes include making their voice louder, suddenly whispering, or talking in a high, squeaky voice or a really low rumble for a sentence or two. All of these things will surprise your brain and help it pay attention to the sound of your teacher's voice.

- If you are listening to music, have an adult help you determine a safe noise level for your ears. This is especially important when using headphones.

- Ask familiar adults (like a parent or teacher) to give you a heads-up before giving directions. This can be something like "I am about to give directions. Ready?" or saying your name to get your attention just before they give directions.

- Use headphones to play music or noise while working. (Ask an adult to listen to the volume and make sure that it is a safe level for your ears. I get that you like the sound loud, but you don't want to damage your hearing!)

## My Executive Strategies - Hearing

My Mode:

Draw an arrow on the Sensory Meter showing where your mode typically is for *hearing*. Then, use the space below to write down some ideas for strategies to help your Brain Security Team out. You can use some examples that are given in the book, but also try to think of new ones!

## Executive Strategies – Taste, Too Much

- Try taking small bites of food rather than whole mouthfuls.
- If you are trying a new food, do it in a calm environment rather than a place where you are feel overwhelmed.
- When trying a new food, first take the time to look at it, smell it, and maybe even touch it.
- Give yourself time to try new foods; don't be in a hurry. It may even take multiple days of attempting to try a new food before you take a bite.
- Plan ahead for what to eat when you will not be home. Doing things like packing a lunch with familiar foods can help you make sure that you have something to eat.
- When trying a new food, have a napkin handy so that you can spit it out if you need to. Also, have something to drink nearby so that you can take a quick sip.

# Executive Strategies – Taste, Not Enough + Seeking

- Ask someone to talk about the flavors of the food while you eat to help you notice them more (for instance, "Wow, this apple is so sweet!" or "There is too much salt in this soup.")

- Try to describe the foods that you are eating and how they taste while you are eating them. If you pair this with the above strategy, you can have a great meal-time discussion about food!

- When you are eating a meal, try to alternate foods; eat a bite of one food and then a bite of a different food to change up the flavors during a meal.

- Trying new foods is a great way to get intense taste input. Your brain doesn't know quite what to expect when tasting something new, so it pays close attention.

- Keep some favorite sauces or spices that you can add to your food to increase the flavor.

- If eating something with an intense flavor helps you to feel more awake, you can use this as a strategy just before or during a sort-of-boring task. For instance, if you start drifting off during math, maybe chew on some intense mint or sour gum during class. (As long as your teacher says yes, of course. If your teacher or school doesn't allow gum, you could try adding flavor to your water.)

## My Executive Strategies - Taste

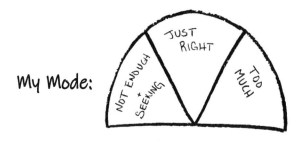

My Mode:

Draw an arrow on the Sensory Meter showing where your mode typically is for **taste**. Then, use the space below to write down some ideas for strategies to help your Brain Security Team out. You can use some examples that are given in the book, but also try to think of new ones!

## Executive Strategies – Smell, Too Much

- Change positions in the room so that you are not close to something that smells a lot, such as an adult's cologne or the garbage can.
- If you are going to be around something that smells bad to you, try using a little bit of a calming scent to override it. You might be able to mist some lavender water on your shirt, for instance.
- If an adult that you are around regularly wears perfume or cologne that bothers you, you can try to ask them politely to wear less or not wear it at all on days when you see them.
- Open the windows in a room to get fresh air if there is an overwhelming smell.
- If you are trying to smell something, like a candle or a perfume sample, wave your hand over it and toward your nose to spread just a little of the smell toward you. You will get less scent doing this than if you put your nose directly up to it.
- If scents of cleaning supplies and detergents bother you, ask the adults in charge to change to a non-scented version.
- If all else fails, you can always try the old-fashioned trick of just plugging your nose.
- If the smell of a food bothers you, try eating it cold instead of warmed up (the warmer a food is, the more smell it will give off!)

## Executive Strategies – Smell, Not Enough + Seeking

- Make a "smell kit." Ask an adult to help you find some safe essential oils that you like the smell of and that smell pretty intense, like peppermint. You can put a drop or two on a cotton ball and keep it in a plastic baggy. Keep these in your desk , locker, or even your pocket so that you have it handy when you need a whiff of something intense!

- Close your eyes when you are smelling something. This blocks out your sense of vision and helps you focus on the smell.

- Just like we did for taste in food, you can ask someone to describe smells and you can try to describe them too.

- Use smells from essential oils or candles while you work.

- Get a few different items to smell, such as an orange, a peppermint, and scented lip balm, and smell them in different orders. The changes in smells will be intense. Use this strategy just before or during a boring task.

- If you are a person who likes to smell different things a lot, take the time to ask an adult, "Is this safe for me to smell?" Some things, like cleaning supplies, could be unhealthy to take a big whiff of.

## My Executive Strategies - Smell

My Mode:

Draw an arrow on the Sensory Meter showing where your mode typically is for *smell*. Then, use the space below to write down some ideas for strategies to help your Brain Security Team out. You can use some examples that are given in the book, but also try to think of new ones!

## Executive Strategies – Touch, Too Much

- Create a space with clear boundaries, maybe using large boxes or a tent, and make a rule that no one is allowed to come in without your permission. When you need a break, you can use this space to get away from anything touching you. Make sure to tell your adult in charge about this so that they can help and so they know what is going on!

- Try wearing gloves or using utensils like a spatula or paintbrush so that you do not have to touch the messy stuff.

- If you are going to touch something messy or if something messy might get on you, keep a napkin nearby so you can clean it off quickly if needed.

- Change positions so that you are in a place where others are less likely to bump into you. This might mean being at the front or back of the line or standing at the edge of a group rather than the center.

- Ask for help to remove tags from clothing or buy "tag-less" clothing.

- If you are shopping for clothing and you like a shirt's look but not the way it feels, try a size up or down and see if it helps.

- When trying to touch a new fabric, try using the back of your hand first instead of the palm of your hand. Did you know that you have fewer touch-detectors on the back of your hand?

- Before doing something like trimming your nails or brushing your teeth, try deep-pressure massaging the area first. More on this later: deep pressure works to kind of calm down your system.

- Put a time or number limit on a task that you don't like the feel of so you know when it will end. For instance, set a timer to brush your teeth or decide that you are only going to trim three fingernails today.

- Try wearing a soft shirt underneath one that feels itchy to you.

## Executive Strategies – Touch, Not Enough + Seeking

- Set up opportunities to intentionally engage in messy play or projects like cooking, painting, or clay modeling. Let yourself get as messy as you want and then clean up.
- Keep fidget items for times when you are supposed to be focusing, like in class.
- Ask a trusted advisor, like your mom or the adult in charge, to help you notice if your clothes are twisted. Instead of having them fix it for you, see if you can figure out what is wrong and describe how it feels before you fix it.
- Get dressed in front of a mirror so you can use your sight to help your touch.
- Make a "feel it" kit that has different textures and things to feel. When you are feeling fidgety or wanting to touch things, grab your kit and go for it!
- Keep an item to feel or fidget with to use in places where you are supposed to keep your hands to yourself, like the fragile dish aisle at the store or a line of people.
- Place Velcro stickers on the bottom of your desk to feel (as long as your teacher says it is okay!)
- Use a textured pencil grip that has bumps or ridges on it for writing.
- Ask people who know you to say your name when touching you on the shoulder or arm to help get your attention.
- If you find that you are always reaching into others' space to feel things, use brightly colored tape to outline your space and then practice keeping your hands and feet inside that space.
- Place paper that you are writing on over a textured surface, like fine sandpaper or grainy wood, so when you write you will feel all of the bumps.

## My Executive Strategies - Touch

My Mode:
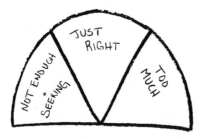

Draw an arrow on the Sensory Meter showing where your mode typically is for **touch**. Then, use the space below to write down some ideas for strategies to help your Brain Security Team out. You can use some examples that are given in the book, but also try to think of new ones!

## Executive Strategies – Vestibular, Too Much

- Try adjusting the speed or size of your movements to help you feel safer. Can you swing and just not go very high? Can you pull off a dance move without feeling sick if you slow it down a bit?

- Hold on! When you are doing something that requires your feet to be off the ground, try holding on to something secure.

- If you don't like tipping your head back to wash your hair, try this: tilt your head back a little bit and pause until you feel comfortable. While you pause, find something to look at in front of you. Keep tilting back a little bit at a time and pausing until your head is in a position where you can wash your hair.

- Hold on again! Another great strategy for tilting your head back is to have something like a shower bar to hold onto. This helps you feel much more stable.

- For motion sickness, try to sit next to a window and keep your gaze way out on the horizon. Looking at something inside the vehicle like a book or phone may make you feel more nauseated.

- When using transportation like a bus or a train, try changing your position so you sit close to the front. The front seat of a car can help, but make sure the adult in charge checks your age to see if the front seat is safe for you.

- If you avoid movement in general, try finding some activities with movement that you are okay with—maybe ballet or walking. It is important to still get exercise!

- Use a stool or adjust your chair so that your feet are securely supported by the stool or the ground.

## Executive Strategies – Vestibular, Not Enough + Seeking

- Schedule time into your day that involves movement.
- Add intense movements to your day. (Remember those tube thingies of the vestibular system from page 19? Think about how you can shake up the water in them a lot!) Movements like jumping, running, and spinning are great.
- When you are doing these types of movements, try making them even more intense. Instead of a regular jump, try jumping high and looking up and then coming down all the way to touch your toes. Or maybe hop on a trampoline so that you get more movement with each jump.
- Use movement right before doing something that requires you to sit still and focus.
- If you have to sit still and focus for a long time, schedule some movement breaks to help wake you up and decrease your fidgets.
- Sit on a ball or a bouncy cushion instead of a regular chair—you can use it to bounce in place and move a little while you sit.
- Ask your teacher if you can stand instead of sitting sometimes during class.
- Try sports that require a lot of fast stopping, starting, and turning, like soccer.
- If you are really wanting to crash into something, create a safe environment and ask a trusted adult to help supervise. Piling up pillows, bean bags, blankets can be a great way to provide a soft landing.
- When deciding what chores you will be responsible for at home or in class, ask for the ones that require you to move around, like taking out the trash, walking the dog, or being the class messenger. This will help give you more movement while you are doing the things that you are supposed to do!

## My Executive Strategies - Vestibular

My Mode:

JUST RIGHT

NOT ENOUGH + SEEKING

TOO MUCH

Draw an arrow on the Sensory Meter showing where your mode typically is for **vestibular** input. Then, use the space below to write down some ideas for strategies to help your Brain Security Team out. You can use some examples that are given in the book, but also try to think of new ones!

## Executive Strategies – Proprioception, Seeking

- Schedule time in your day for movement.
- Add in movements to your day that really get your arms and legs moving in big ways like star jumps.
- Use "heavy work" to make your muscles work extra hard. This involves doing things like carrying heavy things or pushing and pulling something.
- Incorporate jumping into your daily routine—this action uses a lot of force from your muscles to jump up, and then it compresses your joints when you land. Both are great sources of proprioception.
- When sitting in place, place a TheraBand, which is basically like a huge rubber band, around the chair legs so that you can push against it with your feet.
- Do chair push-ups while you sit.
- Get some big squeezes by asking for tight hugs from safe adults, wrapping yourself up tightly in a blanket, or making yourself into a pillow sandwich (have someone put pillows around you and squeeze tight!)
- When deciding what chores you will be responsible for at home or in class, ask for ones that involve carrying, pushing, or pulling things, such as carrying the gym equipment to recess or taking the trash out.
- Wear super-tight clothing that squeezes around you.
- Keep thick putty around so that you can squeeze it with your hands.
- Try sports that require heavy work such as weightlifting, tug-of-war, or wrestling.
- If you are really wanting to crash into something, create a safe environment and ask a trusted adult to help supervise. Piling up pillows, bean bags, blankets can be a great way to provide a soft landing.
- Chew gum or "chewelry."

My Executive Strategies - Proprioception

My Mode:

JUST RIGHT

NOT ENOUGH + SEEKING

TOO MUCH

Draw an arrow on the Sensory Meter showing where your mode typically is for *proprioception*. Then, use the space below to write down some ideas for strategies to help your Brain Security Team out. You can use some examples that are given in the book, but also try to think of new ones!

# Putting These Strategies to Work

That was a lot of strategies! It's time now to get all of this information together, Exec, and put it to work for you. I know it's been a lot of learning, so here is an acronym to help you use all of the information in this book. I call it the NICCCE Action Steps. (Yeah, I know that there are too many C's in that—keep reading, you'll get it.)

Here is what NICCCE stands for:

**N** otice a sensory challenge

**I** dentify what mode you are in and for what sense(s)

**C** ompose a statement describing your Brain Security Team

**C** onsider strategies that can help your Brain Security Team

**C** hoose the best strategy

**E** xecute the best strategy

Let's take a closer look at each of these steps.

# Notice

The first step in managing your Sensory Modes is to notice that you are in a sensory challenge. This means that you are in a mode other than Just Right, so you are getting too much or not enough of some type of sensory input, making it hard for you to do whatever it is you are trying to do.

You may notice overall feelings at first, such as overwhelm, agitation, and lethargy. You might feel checked-out or seek sensory input. On the other hand, you may notice something specific. You may be bothered by the lights or the tags in your clothes, or you might feel sleepy with the teacher's voice sounding like it's underwater, be unable to understand and follow directions, chew on the collar of your shirt, or fidget in your chair.

Looking through your lists of sensory-pattern characteristics may help you start to notice sensory challenges faster. Remember, patterns are things that happen over and over in the same way, so once you have identified a sensory pattern, it is likely to happen that way again. Also, your Chief Advisor and other trusted adults in your life can be super helpful when you are first learning to notice sensory challenges. Ask them to help by pointing out when they think you are experiencing them.

# Identify

Next, it is important to identify exactly which mode you are in and for what sense(s). Are you in Too Much, Not Enough, or Seeking mode? Where are you on your Sensory Meter? And what sense, or senses, are you experiencing this mode in?

# Compose

The third step is to compose a statement the describes the sensory challenge and what your Brain Security Team is doing. Your statement should be something like this:

"My Brain Security Team is not letting in enough vestibular information."

or

"My Brain Security Team is letting in too much touch information."

Because our strategies are aimed at helping our Brain Security Team let in a Just Right amount of sensory info, this statement is going to tell us *exactly* what we need to do to help because it tells us *exactly* what the problem is. And Execs are all about being exact.

## Consider

Consider different strategies that can help your Brain Security Team move your Sensory Meter more toward Just Right. These could be strategies that are listed in the Executive Strategies section, or they could be new strategies that you come up with. Either way, make sure that you are thinking about how to help your security team get either more or less sensory info.

This step is a brainstorm step—try to think of as many different strategies as you can.

## Choose

Now it is time to choose the best strategy out of all of the ideas that you listed. Here are a few questions that can help you to choose the best strategy when you are thinking of all of the ideas that you had.

- Which strategy will be the most effective?
- Do I have the tools that I need to use each strategy?
- Which strategy might be the most appropriate for the setting that I am in?

For example, maybe you need to send more proprioceptive information to your brain and you think of either jumping in place or setting up cushions and jumping down off a sofa onto the cushions. You think that crashing down onto cushions would be more effective because it really gets your brain some good info, but you are currently in the middle of reading class and there is no sofa or cushions available so you don't have the tools to do that. Instead, you choose to do some star jumps because they give a good amount of proprioceptive information and because you can do them in class or out in the hallway (with your teacher's permission, of course).

## Execute

Execute means to put a plan into action, so now, Exec, it's time to do the strategy that you chose! Use whatever strategy that you thought was best and help your Brain Security Team get a Just Right amount of input to your brain.

Ready to give this a try? You will find recording sheets for the NICCCE Action Steps next!

Visit **brainexecutiveprogram.com** to download additional NICCCE Recording Sheets.

# NICCCE Recording Sheet

**Notice**      *What sensory challenges are you noticing? Write about what you are feeling.*

**Identify**      *What sensory mode are you in? For what sense(s)?*

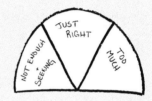

**Compose**      *Write a statement saying what your Brain Security Team is doing.*

**Consider**      *Brainstorm ideas to help move your Sensory Meter toward Just Right.*

**Choose**      *Write down the strategy that you choose and why it is the best.*

**Execute**      *Do it! Put your strategy to work!*

## NICCCE Recording Sheet

Notice

Identify

Compose

Consider

Choose

Execute

## NICCCE Recording Sheet

Notice

Identify

Compose

Consider

Choose

Execute

## NICCCE Recording Sheet

Notice

Identify

Compose

Consider

Choose

Execute

## NICCCE Recording Sheet

Notice

Identify

Compose

Consider

Choose

Execute

## NICCCE Recording Sheet

Notice

Identify

NOT ENOUGH SEEING | JUST RIGHT | TOO MUCH

Compose

Consider

Choose

Execute

Executive Extras

Now that you are an expert on using the NICCCE system, here are a few more things to know.

# Using Multiple Senses Together

We have kind of been talking about each sense separately, which is a really helpful way to think about them to help us organize all of the information and make sure that we understand each part. The thing is, you are never using only one sense at a time. They all work together to help you understand all of the stuff happening around and inside you. For instance, you can *smell* and *taste* buttery popcorn while you are *watching* a movie that you can *hear* the characters talking in, all while *feeling* a blanket snugly wrapped around you and, oh yeah, knowing that you are sitting upright and not upside down (*vestibular*). It all works together.

So what does this mean for managing your Sensory Meter and moving your meter toward Just Right? It means that you can use senses together to help you move your arrow to the right or to the left even better!

Let's pretend that you are a Not Enough or Seeker for vision and you are having trouble focusing on what your teacher is teaching. First, you add in some strategies to help boost your visual input like moving closer to the board and turning the lights on brightly at the front of the room where the board is. Great. Now, how can 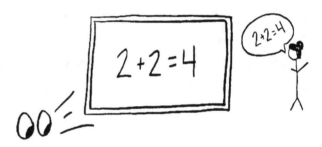 your other senses help? Asking your teacher to read out loud what the board says can use your sense of hearing to help boost your vision. You could also do a few quick jogging laps around the classroom to get your body moving, using your vestibular and proprioceptive systems to add in some wake-up input to your brain (with your teacher's permission, of course). What about adding in some touch? If you are learning about rocks in science, could you ask to hold and feel the rocks that your teacher is talking about? Or maybe if you are in geography, could you have a map right in front of you so that you can touch the places on the map that your teacher is talking about? All of these are great ways to use multiple senses at the same time to support each other and help you work at your best.

What about using this multiple-sense idea if you are a Too Much? Let's say that you are a Too Much-Vestibular, but you really want to skateboard with your friends. You decide to work on this at home with your uncle to help you get used to the feeling of skateboarding. First, you use some of your vestibular strategies, like going slowly to limit movement input.

How can your other senses help? You can start by practicing in a quiet, calm place. You pick an empty parking lot so that there are fewer noises and fewer people and cars moving around. Limiting the sound and visual input can help you feel less overwhelmed. Also, you can use some proprioceptive input like a big bear-hug from your uncle to help calm down your system before you even try getting on the skateboard. If the feeling of clothing bothers you, it can help to take a moment to think about what you are wearing .If you are really bothered by the feeling of tags inside clothing, make sure that you are fully tag-less for this skateboarding adventure. That way your brain won't have to worry about itchy tags while it is also trying to figure out this skateboard thing.

## Patterns in Different Environments and Circumstances

We talked about patterns and how they work—how they are generally the same and are predictable. This is absolutely true, because a pattern is predictable. But at this point, you might be thinking that your patterns aren't always the same or all-the-way predictable. You might find that sometimes during the day you are more likely to be in Just Right mode, while at other times you are more likely to be in Too Much mode. Or maybe some days you are totally a Seeker in geography class, but other days you are a Just Right. Let me explain …

Your brain and security team have some ways in which they typically work—we call these your sensory patterns. But things can influence your sensory patterns and can make you move closer to or further away from Just Right mode. In fact, where you are, what you are doing, what is happening around you, and how many times you've been in the same place doing the same thing all influence your patterns.

Here are a few specifics about things that can influence your sensory modes and patterns.

## The "Newness" of What You Are Doing

Being in a new place, doing a new thing, or having something new happening is a major way in which patterns can be influenced. Your brain pays extra attention whenever there is something new going on.[5] In fact, when something new is happening, your Brain Security Team actually lets in more information about it.[21] This moves your sensory gauge to the right, meaning if you are a Not Enough or Seeker, you feel more Just Right when new things are happening. If you are a Just

Right, you may stay in the Just Right zone but feel more awake and pay more attention, or you may move into the Too Much zone. And if you are already a Too Much, new things may make you feel overwhelmed or anxious.[16] In fact, Too Muches often avoid new things.

How can you use this brainy knowledge to your advantage? If you are a Not Enough or a Seeker, try to add new things into your day to help keep your brain awake and active. On the other hand, if you are a Too Much, try to limit new things, keeping it all in Familiar Land.

**Executive Tip:** *Tell the adults in charge about how new things affect you. They can help to either add more new things into your day or try to keep most things the same. Also, for Too Muches, if something new is going to happen, they can give you a heads-up so you feel more prepared.*

## Habits and Routines

Habits and routines are all about doing things the same way again and again. And doing things the same way is pretty much the opposite of new, so habits and routines help to move your Sensory Meter to the left. Think about this in Brain Exec terms. If you are a Too Much, try to develop and stick to familiar habits and routines. This will help your brain get less new information and keep you more toward a Just Right mode. If you are a Not Enough or a Seeker, try to do things out of order or in new ways. If you usually walk the dog and then do your chores, try shaking things up by doing your chores before walking your dog. Or, if you always eat dinner at the dining room table, try taking it outside for a picnic.

## The Time of Day

Even the time of day can influence your Sensory Modes.[3] Maybe you are a person who has a hard time waking up in the morning, and for the first hour of every day you just feel super sleepy. Sounds like Not Enough mode, right? Well, if you are a Not Enough in the mornings, you could add some exercise and movement or maybe turn on your favorite upbeat tune while you get dressed. Definitely don't plan to finish your algebra homework first thing in the morning.

Sensory Too Muches sometimes notice that they are more likely to be in Too Much mode later in the day. It is as if all of the sensory input throughout the day adds up and you finally get to the point where it is just too much.[16] This might mean that something that doesn't bother you in the morning makes you feel agitated in the afternoon. Perhaps you feel fine listening to music in the car on the way to school, but on the way home, the sound of music really bothers you and you just need quiet for a while. Or maybe you hold it together all day at school, but after school you are tired and sensory things bother you a lot. Maybe you are more likely to start arguing with your parent or the grown-up in charge or you feel anxious after a long day. If this is you, try to schedule in some quiet and calm time after school. Your brain may need a break.

## Stress and Anxiety

Stress and anxiety can also affect how you experience sensory input. During times in which you feel stressed or anxious, your sensory gauge might move more toward the "Too Much" side, making you more likely to feel like sensory input is too much for you.[3] Things that don't typically bother you may agitate you. Things that just annoy you most of the time may start to really overwhelm you. You might feel more like you need to get away from whatever is bothering you, and you might even experience a fight-or-flight response.

What can a Brain Exec do about this? For starters, if you think that you are experiencing stress or anxiety, tell a trusted adult. Also, when you feel anxious, decrease the amount of sensory information around you and take "sensory breaks" in a quiet space. Fortunately, you have lots of strategies to help you do this, Exec.

## Fight or Flight – A Special Section for Sensory Too Much

Remember way back in the book where you first learned about the four different sensory modes? Do you remember a part in the Sensory Too Much section that talked about something called "Fight or Flight"? It had a couple of funny pictures with bears? Well, it's time to revisit that information and learn a little more about it. (Note for Not Enoughs and Seekers: You can skip this section if you want!)

Sometimes when your brain is overwhelmed by sensory information, it thinks that there is a real threat to your safety. Your brain is all about keeping you safe, because, well, if you aren't safe, your brain isn't either. It's basic self-preservation.

When your brain thinks that something is threatening your safety, it sets off an alarm system in your body to help it respond to whatever threat there is.[27,28] In general, if something is trying to get you, what are your options? Run away or fight it off, right? Well, a brainiac scientist, Walter Bradford Cannon, figured this all out way back in 1915. He wanted to have a catchy term; "run away or fight" just didn't do it, so he decided to call it "Fight or Flight," which has a nice ring to it.[22] I guess he was right, because more than 100 years later, people are still talking about it.

***PRO TIP:*** If you decide to be a scientist when you grow up, make sure to name your findings something cool. Then maybe someone will write about you in a book 100 years later.

So, exactly what happens when you are in Fight or Flight mode? Well, first your brain detects something that it thinks is a threat to your safety. Then your brain tells your body to get ready because something bad might be about to happen. How does your body get ready for this? So glad you asked! Here is a list of things that happen in your body during a Fight or Flight response:

- Your heart beats faster and harder so it can send more blood to the muscles in your body to help them work—like the muscles in your legs so that you can run, or the muscles in your arms so you can punch.
- Parts of your lungs temporarily get bigger so that they can take in more oxygen. More oxygen into your lungs means more oxygen to your muscles, helping them to work better!
- The pupils in your eyes get bigger, helping them to take in more light so you can see better.
- Your cells release energy called "glucose" into your bloodstream so that you have more energy to do all of this flighting-and-fighting stuff.
- You start sweating because your brain figures, "Hey, if you are running and jumping and kicking and punching and all, you are going to be getting a workout! Better start sweating to help the body cool down."
- Your stomach and intestines shut down because if you are super busy with a threat, your body doesn't have the time or energy to think about things like food digestion.[22,28]

# Fight or Flight and Sensory Too Much Mode

Okay, but wait, I get all of this if a bear is trying to eat you, but what exactly does it have to do with sensory stuff? To answer this, let's think about the basics of a threat. It's usually something in your environment that could be dangerous (like a snake, a bear, or a cliff) or an activity that you could get hurt doing (like biking too fast or swinging too high). Well, how do you learn about things in your environment and activities? Through your *senses*!! It is your sensory system that is providing the information to your brain about potential threats.

Now let's think about how this is all specifically related to Sensory Too Much mode. When your brain is in Too Much mode, it might activate the system of your brain responsible for responding to threats and engaging in a Fight or Flight response.[3,7,16] Why? Because a Too Much brain detects danger or discomfort where other brains may not.[13] For instance, swinging is something that a lot of kids do, right? If a Too Much-Vestibular tries to swing at a playground, the movements of the swing can be very alarming. Their heart may start to race and they may start breathing quickly. For a Too Much, even swinging small amounts can feel like a gargantuan rollercoaster that is out of control. That's where the brain might step in and say, "Hey! This is not safe!!! We are detecting too much movement here!"

# Workbook Section: Brain Exec Activity

Can you think of times that you have gone into a Fight or Flight response because of sensory input? Write down examples in the space below.

_____

_____

_____

_____

_____

_____

# So what Do You Do about This whole Fight-or-Flight Thing?

Is swinging at a playground a dangerous activity? Not really. But if you *feel* this way on a swing, you aren't going to want to swing much. Does being a Too Much-Vestibular mean you can never swing? Definitely not! For one, you know how to think of some great strategies to help your brain not get too much vestibular info. You could swing slowly, for instance, or you could hold onto the swing's ropes to be more stable. But here's the thing: if you are in a Fight or Flight reaction, you will need a little more support than just the regular strategies that you have already learned about. Why? Because before you do anything else, you need to help your brain and body calm down.

 **Brain Fact:** *Sensory Too Muches who experience a Fight or Flight response need to calm their brains and bodies down before they try any of their other strategies.*
*First: calm your brain and body.*
*Then: implement your sensory specific strategies.*

# How to Calm Down a Fight-or-Flight Response Using Brain Language

We are going to talk some serious brain language now. Your brain and body are always communicating to help them work together. It's easy to know how your brain tells your body things, like "Hey, move your right arm," or "Time to grab your science book and turn to page 93." But don't forget that your body also talks to your brain. I am going to say that again because it's important: *Your body also talks to your brain.* This is how your brain knows what is going on in your body and how to feel about it.[29]

One example of this is the feeling of hunger. Detectors in your body notice that you haven't eaten in a while, your stomach is empty, and you need some energy. So they send a signal to your brain about all of this, and your brain goes, "Hey! I must be hungry! I should probably find some food."

Your body also tells your brain about other things that it is feeling. How? Through things like what your muscles are doing, how your heart is working, and how you are breathing.[29] Have you ever watched a scary movie and you are waiting for something bad to happen, like a monster

popping out? Think about what your body is doing at this time. Your muscles are probably tense and tight. Your heart is pounding fast and hard. You are probably breathing quickly, and your eyes are wide. You may not know it, but all the while, detectors throughout your body are sending your brain information about all of this. So your brain goes, "Well, my muscles are tight and tense, my heart is pounding, and I am breathing fast … Hey! This all sounds like those things that happen during a Fight or Flight response. I must be scared! I'd better start feeling scared."

Now for the good news! When your body is relaxed and happy, it also sends signals to your brain about how it feels. If you are kicked back on your couch, your muscles are relaxed, your heart is beating normally, and you are breathing deeply and slowly … your brain gets all of these signals and goes, "Wow, I seem very relaxed and content. I must be feeling pretty good and safe and calm."

Are you ready for the best news of all? You can use this brain-body language to tell your brain how to feel![28] If you are a Sensory Too Much and are experiencing stress, anxiety, or a fight or flight response, it is super important that you do this. In fact, you should do this *first*, before you even start to use one of your strategies to help your brain security team.

## Brain Language Hacks to Help You Calm Down

So exactly how do you get your body to tell your brain to calm down? It's all about doing some specific things. Here are three techniques to help your body tell your brain that everything is okay and that it can calm down.

### *Breathing*

Adjusting how you breathe is probably the #1 way to get your body to tell your brain to calm down. You need to know just a little anatomy to understand how this works. Inside your body are your lungs, which are like two big balloons that fill with air every time you take a breath. Just underneath your lungs is this big muscle called a diaphragm that your lungs sit on. If you take a big, deep breath and fill your lungs with air, it moves that diaphragm-muscle thing down toward your belly. When that muscle moves down in your belly, it tells your brain to calm down.[29,30] I am not making this up; it's true.

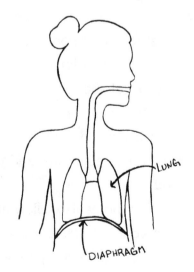

Here's the tricky part. You can fill your lungs up at the top so that your chest moves out and your shoulders move up. The problem with this way of breathing is that it doesn't move your diaphragm down. When you are using breathing to calm your body and brain, it is important to take the air into your lungs slowly and think about moving all of that air down toward your belly button. When you do this, your belly should actually get bigger because all the air makes it stick out. In fact, we often call this trick "Belly Breathing."

One of the best things about Belly Breathing is that you can use it anywhere. If you start feeling a Fight or Flight response, say, in the middle of class or at a store, you can start to belly-breathe, and no one around you will even notice!

## *Deep Pressure Touch and Proprioception*

Our senses of proprioception and touch are our buddies during Fight or Flight responses because they can help us to calm down.[31,32] To use touch for calming, we don't use just any kind of touch; we use a specific kind called "deep pressure touch." This kind of touch happens when your skin is rubbed or squeezed firmly, like a massage. Things like tight hugs, massage from a trusted adult, tight clothing that squeezes around you, wrapping yourself up super snugly in a blanket, using a weighted blanket, or doing some self-massage like squeezing and rubbing your arms are all ways to get deep pressure touch.

What about proprioception? Proprioception for calming is a little different from the kind we tell Seekers to use. Instead of doing things like jumping and crashing, use strong squeezes and stretches. Try giving yourself a really tight hug and holding it or doing some yoga stretches.

## *Relaxing Your Muscles*

When you are in a fight-or-flight response, your muscles tense up and tighten, getting ready to run away or fight. This tightening of the muscles informs your brain that you are worried about something. Luckily, doing the exact opposite can tell your brain that everything is okay and that it can calm down.[29,33] What is the opposite of tense? Relaxed!

To use this strategy, relax your muscles on purpose. There are a few ways to do this; it's usually best to try them all and decide which one you like best. One way to relax your muscles is to first squeeze all of your muscles as tightly as you can, hold it for a count of 10, and then relax them, letting them feel nice and loose. Allow them to feel relaxed and loose for at least a full minute and then repeat this exercise if you want.

Another way to do this is to think about a specific area of your body and let all of the muscles there relax. You can start with somewhere like your foot and then add in sections of your body to work up your leg, then your stomach and back, your arms, and finally your neck and head until your whole body is relaxed. People call this strategy "progressive muscle relaxation." Other people like to lie flat on their backs and just let all of their muscles relax at the same time. Try out different ways and decide what you like best, Exec. Also, think about what kind of strategy you can use wherever you are. For instance, if you are at home you may be able to lie on your back and relax, but that might be hard to do at school. If you need to relax your muscles at school, try learning a system that you can use while sitting at your desk.

*PRO TIP:* when you are finished relaxing all of your muscles, try to move slowly for a while and stay relaxed.

# Wake Up, Brain! – A Section for Not Enoughs and Seekers

Here is a part for all of you Not Enoughs and Seekers out there. Let's talk a little more about your RAS and what it's doing in your brainstem. Remember, the RAS's job is to notice when sensory information is coming in and then shout up to the brain to wake it up and get it ready to take in the information.[3,5,9] All of this shouting by the RAS helps to keep your brain feeling awake, alert, and active during the day when things are happening around you and you are busy doing fantastic stuff. Which is great, but if you are in Not Enough or Seeking mode and your Brain Security Team is blocking out too much sensory input, your RAS isn't getting much. And you, Exec, already know the story when this happens: the RAS doesn't tell the brain to be awake and alert, the brain starts getting bored and tired, and you start feeling lethargic, bored, checked-out, or sleepy.

There are definitely times that we want to feel sleepy, like nighttime. But there are other times when we do not want to feel sleepy. I could be wrong here, but I am thinking that during activities like science class, family meals, conversations with friends, or important events, you probably don't want to be falling asleep or feeling super lethargic. Not Enoughs and Seekers often feel this way, even during times when it would be helpful to feel awake and alert.[16] Well, I have some good news for you, Exec. You can use your brainy knowledge and a few strategies to get some sensory info to your RAS so that it can help your brain feel awake and alert!

## Workbook Section: Brain Exec Activity

Can you think of times that you often feel sleepy, lethargic, bored, or checked out during the day? Write down some examples in the space below.

_____

_____

_____

_____

_____

_____

_____

_____

_____

# Helping Your Brain Feel More Awake and Alert

Helping a Not Enough or Seeker brain feel more awake and alert is all about knowing your security team and helping it out. If you are feeling lethargic, bored, checked-out, or sleepy at times during the day when others seem to be awake and alert, your Sensory Meter is reading on the left side and your Brain Security Team is blocking out too much sensory information.

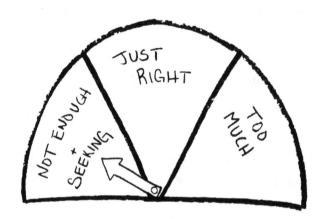

I bet you already guessed what a Brain Executive can do about this. Get more sensory input to your RAS and brain! The ideas listed on the Executive Strategy pages are a great start because they are all ways to send more sensory info to your brain. Don't forget that every bit of sensory input that reaches your RAS means that your brain gets a little "wake up and pay attention!" message.[3,9] So every time you add stuff to see, hear, taste, smell, or feel, your brain wakes up a little. This is a great time to take another look at those strategy pages and think about what sensory input you can add to your day to help your brain wake up. I'll wait here …

# Super-Charged Wake-Ups for Your Brain

All of those strategies are fantastic ways to help your brain feel more awake and alert, but a few in particular are extra-good at doing this. Here are some of my favorite brain wake-ups:

### *Intense Vestibular*

Get up and move, Exec! Your vestibular system is a powerful brain waker-upper. Taking a movement break can really help to wake up a sleepy brain. So go ahead and jump, run, spin, twirl, swing, dance, or whatever else you can think of to get that body moving. Remember that fluid in your vestibular tubes? Try to really shake it up as much as you can!

### *Chewing on Something Chewy or Crunchy*

Chewing on something really crunchy, or tough and chewy, gets the muscles in your mouth and jaw working overtime. This sends lots of proprioceptive information up to your brain. Try some extra-hard gum, tough jerky, fruit leather, crunchy chips, or a crisp apple to wake your brain up.

### *Extreme Tastes*

While you're chewing on something, throw in some wild tastes to help wake up your brain. Try super sour, intensely sweet, rockin' ranch, or maybe spice it up some!

### *Cold*

Cold temperature is also a super-charged wake-up for your brain. Try sipping on some ice-cold water, splashing your face with cold water, or, if you are brave enough, jumping in a cold shower. Brrrrrrrrr.

*Exec, we are getting to the end of the book. It's been an awesome journey. There are just a few more things that you should know ...*

## Embrace the Patterns that Make You, You!

All of this talk about helping your brain move toward Just Right mode might have started to make you think that being in Just Right mode is the right way to be, all the time, for everyone. But here is the thing: THAT'S NOT TRUE!

I know I have already said this multiple times, but it is really important, so here it is again:

## *All sensory patterns and modes are great. They each have strengths and challenges, and none is better than the others.*

And this is a perfect time to take a look at modes, patterns, and you being awesome ...

# Executive Explanation
# Modes, Patterns, and the Awesomeness That Is YOU

We have talked about modes and patterns a lot; they work together closely, so it can get confusing. Are they the same thing? No, but they are very similar. Your modes work together to make your patterns. Let me explain …

Like we said before, your sensory *mode* is how your Brain Security Team is working *at any point in time* to allow sensory information up to your brain. This means your brain could be getting a Just Right amount of sensory information, Too Much, or Not Enough, or it might be Seeking more. Your sensory *patterns* are made up by what modes you are *usually* in. If your Brain Security Team *usually* lets in too much sound information, you have a sensory pattern of being a Too Much for hearing. If you Brain Security team *usually* blocks out too much touch information, you have a sensory pattern of being a Not Enough for touch. Remember, patterns are something that happen the same way over and over again.

Here is the key point: We want to move your sensory *mode* toward Just Right when being in Too Much, Not Enough, or Seeking mode makes it hard to do what you want and need to do. This doesn't mean that you should always try to be a Just Right; it just means that if you are having a hard time doing something because of how your Brain Security Team is working, then we want to help it work a little better, move you toward Just Right, and get you back to working at being amazing.

On the other hand, we don't really try to change your sensory *patterns* because they are part of what makes you *you*, and you are pretty incredible, so we don't want to change that. Being an Exec is more about *understanding* your sensory patterns than changing them. And when you understand them, it can help you to understand yourself and help your awesome self to work a little better sometimes.

So to recap that super-important point: Modes are how your Brain Security Team is working at any point in time. No mode is better or worse than any other, but if you are in a mode that is making it hard to do whatever it is that you are trying to do, then we can help your brain move toward Just Right mode so you can do the task.

Patterns are they ways in which your modes usually happen. We don't try to change your patterns, because they make you, you. Understanding your patterns is super important though, and if while in your patterns you find yourself in a mode that is making life hard for a bit, then we can try to move your mode toward Just Right. Make sense, Exec?

# *Your Sensory Patterns make you, you and the world only has one you, so be the You-iest You that you can be!*

## Workbook Activity:
## Brain Exec Activity – Modes and Patterns

Let's look at how this mode/pattern relationship works for you. Below, write down one of your sensory patterns that is anything other than Just Right. Write down what sense it is for and what your pattern is:

Sense: _____        Pattern: _____

Then, write down a few things that are awesome about that pattern. How does it make you *you*? Has it ever helped you be extra-good at something? List some great things about your pattern.

_____

_____

_____

_____

_____

Now, think about a specific time that being in that mode made it difficult to do something. (Note here that since we are talking about a *specific time*, we are shifting over to talking about a mode.) What were you doing? How did the mode work in that moment? What about that made it difficult?

_____

_____

_____

_____

_____

_____

Imagine if you had been able to help your Brain Security Team move toward a Just Right mode in that moment. How would doing so have helped you?

_____

_____

_____

_____

_____

_____

And don't forget: even though we may adjust our _mode_ for a little bit, that doesn't mean we are trying to change our _patterns_!

Soooooo …

If you are a Seeker, keep on having lots of energy, bouncing through life, and wanting to touch and taste and feel everything. You are fun and bright and always up for anything! If at times you find it difficult to do something like paying attention in math class because you just want to be up and moving, use some sensory strategies to move toward Just Right and help you through math. And while you are masterfully solving math problems, keep on loving life!

If you are a Not Enough, keep on being a chill, calm, nothing-bothers-me kind of person. You are amazing for your ability to be relaxed in the wildest of circumstances. When everyone else is kind of freaking out, they can count on you to be the calm, no-worries person. If at times you struggle to stay awake and alert during important things like listening to directions, use some sensory strategies to move toward Just Right and help you listen and follow directions when needed. And keep on being that relaxed kid with the chill vibe.

If you are a Too Much, keep on being that alert and attentive person who always notices things before others do. You are awesome for your ability to detect what others don't notice or to notice them first. Is this a superpower? If at times you experience challenges because you are overwhelmed or anxious about all of the sensory information happening around and inside you, use some sensory strategies to help you move toward Just Right. And keep on being the person who is always noticing the amazing things around them and helping others notice them too.

If you are a Just Right, keep on doing whatever it is that you want and need to do while you can use all of your senses at their best abilities. It is pretty cool that you can go from energetically running around the bases during a kickball tournament to sitting in English class reading Shakespeare to laughing with all of your friends at lunch. If at times you move over into Too Much or Not Enough mode and it makes it difficult for you to do whatever it is that you are doing, use some sensory strategies to help shift you back over into Just Right. And keep on being that kid who can match whatever they are doing and do it so well.

Whoever you are, Exec,

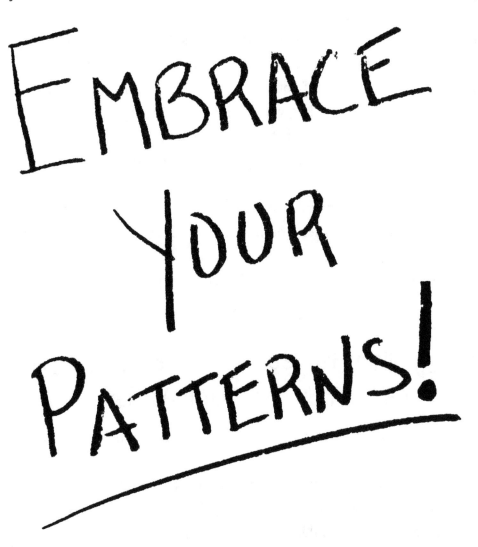

# When You Might Need a Little More Help

Every good Exec knows when to seek the help of an expert advisor. I'm not sure if you've noticed, but sensory modulation can be complicated. I mean, we have been learning *neuroscience*, after all. Fortunately, there is an entire group of professionals who help people with sensory modulation challenges find ways to get to Just Right mode. After reading this book, if you and your Chief Advisor still have questions or are having a hard time figuring out exactly what your patterns are and how they are operating in your everyday life, this might be a good time to ask one of these professionals to be a personal executive advisor. Also, if you are reading this book and you are thinking, "Whoa! Some of these challenges totally describe me, and they are making it really hard to do things that I want and need to do every day!" then that is also a good time to find one of those professionals.

Everyone has sensory systems that work to tell them about the world around and inside them. And everyone's sensory systems are challenged sometimes by having not enough or too much input. This is all part of being human. Which I am guessing you are. (Note: If you are an alien reading this book, will you please post a review and let me know about it? Who knows, maybe I will make it to the top of the Alien Bestseller list!)

Sensory patterns can become a problem when they get in the way of doing everyday things that you want and need to do.[14] If you find that you are often a Too Much, Not Enough, or Seeker and it is making it hard to do things like hanging out with friends, playing a sport, going to a store, or paying attention in class, then you might want to find a professional sensory expert to be an advisor.

(Some of you may be reading this book with a sensory pro, and if so, you can go ahead and high-five yourself.)

# Knowing When to Seek Direct Professional Help (A Section for Chief Advisors)

Here is a section just for the Chief Advisors reading this book and helping out a super-great Brain Exec.

First of all, shout-out to the parents, grandparents, foster parents, aunts, uncles, teachers, mentors, coaches, or any other trusted caregiver reading this book with your Brain Exec. The experts here at the Brain Executive Program think you are amazing!

As mentioned before, everyone has sensory systems, and everyone experiences sensory-based challenges at times, so how do you know when your Exec needs more help? Sensory challenges become a "dysfunction" when they interfere with daily life.[14] If you find that your child is regularly having difficulty participating in school, family routines, events, social activities, extracurricular activities, or other everyday activities, and you suspect that sensory-based challenges are contributing to this difficulty, then you may benefit from seeking direct professional support. Also, if after reading this book you still feel confused about aspects of sensory modulation and how they specifically relate to your child, find a professional who can provide personalized and direct support.

A good guideline: when in doubt, ask! Discuss your concerns with your child's pediatrician or family physician and ask for their guidance. You may also call and describe your concerns to a local pediatric therapy clinic, where sensory-based therapists (often occupational therapists) are on staff. Ask for their professional opinion on whether an evaluation is needed. In addition, school systems can be a great resource. Schools have therapists and counselors on staff to address issues that interfere with learning and classroom participation. If you suspect that sensory-based challenges are impacting your child's participation and performance at school, discuss your concerns with your child's teachers and educational staff and ask if they think that an evaluation is needed.

# An Executive Wrap-Up

Congrats, Exec! You made it to the end of the book, and you are now officially a Sensory-Smart Brain Executive! You know all about sensory everything and how to help your brain get a Just Right amount of sensory info.

Remember that KWL chart from the very beginning of the book? It's finally time to finish it! Go back and see what you wrote. What were the things that you wanted to know? Did you learn all of them? In the "L" section, write down what you learned.

# Workbook Section:
# Brain Exec Activity

My favorite part about this book is:

_____

_____

_____

The most useful thing that I learned is:

_____

_____

_____

Here are a few things that I do differently now because I understand my sensory patterns:

_____

_____

_____

*And that is it, Exec! It's been a great journey, and I hope that you have enjoyed it. Now go use your new superpower to conquer the world (for good, of course)!*

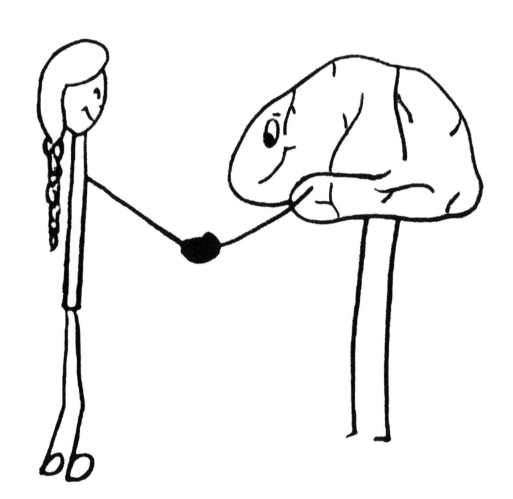

# References

1. Bundy, Anita C., and Colleen Hacker. "The Art of Therapy." In *Sensory Integration Theory and Practice 3rd Edition*, edited by Anita C. Bundy & Shelly J. Lane, 286–299. Philadelphia: F.A. Davis Company, 2020.

2. Brown, Anahita, Tamara Tse, and Tracy Fortune. "Defining Sensory Modulation: A Review of the Concept and a Definition for Application by Occupational Therapists." *Scandinavian Journal of Occupational Therapy* 26 no. 7 (2019).

3. Lane, Shelly J. "Sensory Modulation Functions and Disorders." In *Sensory Integration Theory and Practice 3rd Edition*, edited by Anita C. Bundy & Shelly J. Lane, 151–180. Philadelphia: F.A. Davis Company, 2020.

4. Blanche, Erna Imperatore, Gustavo Reinoso, and Dominique Blanche Kiefer. "Using Clinical Observations within the Evaluation Process." In *Sensory Integration Theory and Practice 3rd Edition*, edited by Anita C. Bundy & Shelly J. Lane, 222–242. Philadelphia: F.A. Davis Company, 2020.

5. Lane, Shelly J., Jessica Zinder Lynn, and Stacey Reynolds. "Sensory Modulation: A Neuroscience and Behavioral Overview." *OT Practice* 15, no. 21 (2010).

6. Kilroy, Emily, Lisa Aziz-Zadeh, and Sharon Cermak. "Ayres Theories of Autism and Sensory Integration Revisited: What Contemporary Neuroscience Has to Say." *Brain Sciences* 9, no. 68 (2019). doi:10.3390/brainsci9030068

7. Lane, Shelly J., Zoe Mailloux, Sarah Schoen, Anita Bundy, Teresa A. May-Benson, L. Diane Parham, Susanne Smith Roley, and Roseann C. Schaff. "Neural Foundations of Ayres Sensory Integration." *Brain Sciences 9* (2019): 153. doi: 10.3390/brainsci9070153

8. Green, Shulamite A., Leanna Hernandez, Susan Bookheimer, and Mirella Dapretto. "Salience Network Connectivity in Autism is Related to Behavioral Markers of Sensory Over-Responsivity." *Journal of American Academy of Child and Adolescent Psychiatry* 55, no. 7 (2016).

9. Siegel, Allan, and Hreday N. Sapru. "The Reticular Formation." In *Essential Neuroscience 4th Edition*, 445–464. Philadelphia: Wolters Kluwer, 2019.

10. Bundy, Anita C., and Stacey Szklut. "The Science of Intervention: Creating Direct Intervention from Theory." In *Sensory Integration Theory and Practice 3rd Edition*, edited by Anita C. Bundy & Shelly J. Lane, 300–337. Philadelphia: F.A. Davis Company, 2020.

11. Bundy, Anita C., and Shelly J. Lane. "Sensory Integration: A. Jean Ayres' Theory Revisited." In *Sensory Integration Theory and Practice 3rd Edition*, edited by Anita C. Bundy & Shelly J. Lane, 2–20. Philadelphia: F.A. Davis Company, 2020.

12. Dunn, Winnie. "Sensory Profile 2: User's Manual." Bloomington: Pearson, 2014.

13. Parham, Diane, and Zoe Mailloux. "Sensory Integration." In *Occupational Therapy for Children and Adolescents 7th Edition*, edited by Jane Case-Smith & Jane Clifford O'Brien, 258-303. St. Louis: Elsevier, Inc., 2015.

14. Miller, Lucy J., Sarah A. Schoen, Shelly Mulligan, and Jullian Sullivan. "Identification of Sensory Processing and Integration Symptom Clusters: A Preliminary Study." *Occupational Therapy International* 2876080 (2017). https://doi.org/10.1155/2017/2876080

15. Schoen, Sarah A., Lucy J. Miller, and Jillian C. Sullivan. "Measurement in Sensory Modulation: The Sensory Processing Scale Assessment." *American Journal of Occupational Therapy* 68, no. 5 (September/ October 2014): 522–530. http://dx.doi.org/10.5014/ajot.2014.012377

16. Miller, Lucy J., Marie E. Anzalone, Shelly J. Lane, Sharon A. Cermak, and Elizabeth T. Osten. "Concept Evolution in Sensory Integration: A Proposed Nosology for Diagnosis." *The American Journal of Occupational Therapy* 61, no. 2 (March/April 2007): 135–140. https://doi.org/10.5014/ajot.61.2.135

17. Bundy, Anita C., and Kim Bulkeley. "Using Sensory Integration Theory in Coaching." In *Sensory Integration Theory and Practice 3rd Edition*, edited by Anita C. Bundy & Shelly J. Lane, 393–422. Philadelphia: F.A. Davis Company, 2020.

18. Lane, Shelley J., Anita C. Bundy, and Michael E. Gorman. "Composing a Theory: An Historical Perspective." In *Sensory Integration: Theory and Practice 3rd Edition*, edited by Anita C. Bundy & Shelly J. Lane, 40-55. Philadelphia: F.A. Davis Company, 2019.

19. Parham, Diane L., Cheryl L. Ecker, Heather Kuhaneck, Diana A. Henry, and Tara J. Glennon. "Sensory Processing Measure, Second Edition. Manual." Torrance: Western Psychological Services, 2021.

20. Su, Chia-Ting, and L. Diane Parham. "Validity of Sensory Systems as Distinct Constructs." *American Journal of Occupational Therapy* 68, no. 5 (2014): 546. http://doi.org/10.5014/ajot.2014.012518

21. Lane, Shelly J. "Structure and Function of the Sensory Systems." In *Sensory Integration: Theory and Practice 3rd Edition*, edited by Anita C. Bundy & Shelly J. Lane, 58–114. Philadelphia: F.A. Davis Company, 2020.

22. White, Leonard E., and William C. Hall. "The Visceral Motor System." In *Neuroscience 6th Edition*, edited by Dale Purves, George J. Augustine, David Fitzpatrick, William C. Hall, Antho- ny-Samuel LaMantia, Richard D. Mooney, Michael L. Platt, and Leonard E. White, 465–488. New York: Oxford University Press, 2018.

23. "Addressing Sensory Integration and Sensory Processing Disorders Across the Lifespan: The Role of Occupational Therapy." American Occupational Therapy Association, 2015. https://www.aota.org/-/media/Corporate/Files/AboutOT/Professionals/WhatIsOT/CY/Fact-Sheets/UDL%20fact%20sheet. Pdf

24. Geddie, Brooke E., Bina, Michael J., and Marijean M. Miller. "Vision and Visual Impairment" in *Children with Disabilities, 7th Edition*, edited by Mark L. Batshaw, Nancy J Roisen, and Gaetano R. Lotrecchiano, 169–188. Baltimore: Paul H Brookes Publishing Company, 2013.

# References

25. Lane, Shelly J., and Stacey Reynolds. "Sensory Discrimination Functions and Disorders." In *Sensory Integration Theory and Practice 3rd Edition*, edited by Anita C. Bundy & Shelly J. Lane, 181–205. Philadelphia: F.A. Davis Company, 2020.

26. Parham, L. Diane, and Joanna Cosbey. "Sensory Integration in Everyday Life." In *Sensory Integration Theory and Practice 3rd Edition*, edited by Anita C. Bundy & Shelly J. Lane, 21–39. Philadelphia: F.A. Davis Company, 2020.

27. Ledoux, Joseph. "Anxious." New York: Viking, 2015.

28. Siegel, Allan, and Hreday N. Sapru. "The Autonomic Nervous System." In *Essential Neuroscience 4th Edition*, 413–444. Philadelphia: Wolters Kluwer, 2019.

29. Korb, Alex. "The Upward Spiral: Using Neuroscience to Reverse the Course of Depression One Small Change at a Time." Oakland: New Harbinger Publications, Inc., 2015.

30. Bordoni, Bruno, Shahin Purgol, Annalisa Bizzarri, Maddalena Modica, and Bruno Morabito. "The influence of breathing on the central nervous system." *Cureus* 10, no. 6, Article e2724 (2018). doi: 10.7759/cureus.2724

31. Chen, Hsin-Yung, Hsiang Yang, Huang-Ju Chi, and Hsin-Ming Chen. "Physiological Effects of Deep Touch Pressure on Anxiety Alleviation: The Weighted Blanket Approach." *Journal of Medical and Biological Engineering* 33, no. 5 (2013).

32. Reynolds, Stacey, Shelly J. Lane, and Brian Mullen. "Effects of Deep Pressure Stimulation on Physiological Arousal." *The American Journal of Occupational Therapy* 69, 6903350010. http://dx.doi.org/10.5014/ajot.2015.015560

33. Pittman, Catherine M., and Elizabeth M. Karle. "Rewire Your Anxious Brain." Oakland: New Harbinger Publications, Inc., 2015.

Printed in the USA
CPSIA information can be obtained
at www.ICGtesting.com
JSHW061215161023
50104JS00001B/1